THE BLISS OR "DISS" CONNECTION?

EMAIL ETIQUETTE

FOR THE
BUSINESS PROFESSIONAL

by: Cherie Kerr

Illustrations by: Jim Doody

Permissions Department, ExecuProv,
DePietro Performance Center
809 N. Main Street, Santa Ana, CA 92701

ExecuProv Press

Printed in the United States of America

First Edition

ISBN # 0-9765970-3-9
ISBN # 978-0-9765970-3-2

For...
    Cameron, Brendan, Tianna and Cashel

ACKNOWLEDGEMENTS

A big thank you to all of those who took the time to answer my survey questions. Their input was invaluable.

I thank my sister, Heather, who, now and so many other times in my life, has been an inspiration to me. She has continuously helped me to further what I consider to be my life's work.

I thank Kate Braniff, Tracy Gibbs, Annie Scranton, Diane Danielson, Harry Husted, Seth Hishmeh, Keith Dugger, Dr. Mark Goulston, Laurie Brown, Drake Doremus and Richard Bartolic for spending time (by email) to share their most personal feelings about email. Without them, I would not have been able to add validity to theory.

I thank Joy Parker for her thoughtful edit. Without her suggestions and pointers, the book may not have hung together as well as I had hoped.

My deep appreciation to Chris Brame. He is sharp, and the depth of his caring is apparent in all his work. This is another book I would not have been able to complete without him.

Thanks to the L.A. Groundlings and the Orange County Crazies sketch and improvisational comedy organizations. In their own way, each has helped me both define and refine my communication techniques and theories.

I am always blessed to have the encouragement of author Gus Lee—a leader, a mentor, a believer and a treasured friend.

I thank my diligent and gentle personal assistant, Jennifer

Lee. My life would not work without her. Diolisa Oyas, too. What a joy to work with you!

I thank my dear friend Patrick Lewis who continually keeps me on the right course.

I thank Dick Frattali, Shirley Prestia, Aileen Braun and Karen Gallinger for helping me teach my classes.

Much appreciation to cartoonist Jim Doody, whose creations really hit the mark.

I thank my many clients who have allowed me to forge positive and meaningful business relationships with them, especially by email.

I thank my parents, Margaret and Charlie. I will never stop missing you.

I continue to cherish the girls from Arcadia High. They are my safety net.

Naturally, I thank sons Keith, Sean and Drake, my daughter Shannon and my precious grandchildren, Cameron, Brendan, Tianna and Cashel.

I thank God for good health and a passion for my work. For the responsibilities He has assigned me, I remain humbled.

THE BLISS OR "DISS" CONNECTION?

Email Etiquette

for the
Business Professional

Table of Contents

"Etiquette in cyberspace is like gravity...there is none."

Introduction

SOMBODY SAVE US!
From technology? No, from ourselves when using it.

For some time I had been mulling over content ideas for my next communications book for the business professional; one dealing with the need for email etiquette. But somehow I couldn't quite buckle down to write it.

As a communications specialist, it was becoming more and more apparent to me that corporate America desperately needed some kind of email rulebook outlining definitive boundaries as to what was good manners and what was not. There was no question that the workforce was running amuck with this remarkable technological advancement. I'd heard horror stories galore from my students—about both sending and receiving emails. I, too, had my own issues, but I was managing. That is, until the day I was sitting in an airport in Philly waiting for a plane, doing one last check in on my PDA to see what my secretary had left me in the way of a daily email roundup. (I didn't want to go through all of them myself while out of town, so she usually did that for me and reported in.) This time, in cryptic bullet form, she led with: "Only a few items." I was glad. The loudspeaker had called my row. I was in a hurry.

As I powered through her report, this is what I read: "You got one from John Mott, asking if you could meet him

Tuesday. He needs help coming up with a theme for his sales presentation. Wants to know if 2 p.m. works for you?" Next bullet: "Bob Reed says he's referred you to an Alice Walters. Her organization needs communication skills training. May need some PR consulting, too. Told her we could help with that. Asked that you call her tomorrow. Told her you would." Next: "Janet wants you to meet her at Quatro Café on Friday, noon or a little earlier, to avoid the lunch crunch. Says she has a possible new client for you." Okay, all good stuff. But as that Cuisinart device began to suck up my boarding pass she dropped the bomb: "Your sister said she got a call from your cousin Michele. Her husband, Ron, died suddenly from a heart attack yesterday. She's devastated. Heather said to call when you can."

I couldn't read the next one. I couldn't wrap my head around the terrible news, nor could I grasp my secretary's nonchalance in passing Heather's email message on to me. No point in reading any further as I headed down the gateway plank. I couldn't concentrate.

I took my seat and tried to assimilate the news. I couldn't call anybody. I couldn't find out what had happened. I couldn't query my sister; couldn't console my cousin. I was strapped to a seat in an Airbus ready to take off on a five-hour flight to the West Coast. Ironic, I thought. I was just leaving the city of Brotherly Love where I had given a passionate keynote speech about the blissful wonders of technology, especially email. But I had also cautioned my audience that email needed some special consideration because it seemed that some corporate types—and even those in our personal lives—were seriously abusing it.

No kidding. My secretary's and sister's emails had proved that!

As I reflected on the observations I'd made in my earlier motivational talk, I began to line them up against what had just happened to me. Dull and frozen, I sat with those thoughts for what seemed like forever, but we hadn't even begun taxying down the runway. I didn't know who I was more mad at, my sister (by far one of the most sensitive and compassionate people I know), or my secretary. Or just email in general.

I didn't want to share my misery with the person seated next to me. I was busy grieving. He didn't know my cousin Michele or her husband Ron, so what could he possibly say? Besides, as I heard the announcement about having to turn off our portable electronic devices, I noticed that he was buried in his computer screen. Hurriedly, he put his laptop away, but I could see his mind was still in it.

I used to think it was rather impersonal to call and give someone bad news, that maybe it was best to do that in person. I also used to think that leaving voice mail messages of a pressing, sensitive or dire nature was tacky, but I suddenly longed for that. At least you could hear the concern or compassion in the messenger's voice.

I stared into my lap, wondering to myself: *Just how* did *we get to the point where we now obit by email*? For God's sakes, where *had* we gone wrong?

Though my body remained practically motionless as I sunk deeply into my just-in-case floatation cushion device, my mind began to get fired up about this book. In a sudden epiphany, I finally realized that those of us using email were engaged in a sort of technological anarchy. No decorum. No rules. No etiquette. Just a freewheeling, put it out there, what the heck, communicate-any-way-you-want-through-the-Internet mentality.

Email was fast becoming the Frisbee toss of cyberspace!

I was trying to draw parallels—grab onto some kind of analogy to illustrate my point in terms of the absurdity of it all. I finally deduced that having no set protocol for email use was akin to passing out automobiles to anyone who felt like driving one, but not giving out that vehicle code book, the one that clearly defines the rules of the road. I pondered what the outcome might have been had none of us been given that thin little DMV pamphlet; the one that instructs us as to the do's and don'ts of the roadways. Let's see: maybe stop and go when you feel like it. Change lanes on a whim. Park where you find space, any space. And, on any given day, pick the side of the road that strikes your fancy. As a consequence, undoubtedly, there would be many more accidents, injuries and, yes, even deaths. Well, I decided, the same holds true of reckless emailing. No faster way to broadside, or altogether kill, a good business relationship than through careless or "lawless" email exchanges.

"This is nuts!" I finally said out loud as we passed over what I guessed was Chicago.

"What?" The computer addict next to me said.

I had forgotten he could hear me. I covered by saying, "Want more *nuts*?" I held up my chintzy in-flight "gourmet nut mix."

"Sure. Thanks," he said.

Though we were inches apart, we didn't communicate at all again until we were over Palm Springs. He remained eye-deep into his computer screen. Me, I scribbled frantically, making notes on what I intended to include in my email etiquette book.

***

Having attended parochial school, I'm big on rules (though I rebelled against most of them from time to time) because they at least give us parameters and a sense of right from wrong. Based on my research, I think I present some pretty solid protocol in the following chapters. If nothing more, I at least want to introduce you to what I consider to be an email "value system." After that, you can draw your own conclusions as to how you want to handle your email communication. But my goal in this book is to at least get you thinking.

Here is the first thing I want you to think about: the state of your relationships. That is the underlying theme throughout this book. How solid and good are your professional relationships? Do you mainly communicate via email as opposed to phoning or meeting people face to face? Why?

***

One reason I'm writing this book is that I have been a communications professional since the 70s. I own a P.R. firm and I also own ExecuProv, a company that teaches eleven different classes to Fortune 500 companies to help them become more effective and interesting public speakers and one-on-one communicators. Out of sheer frustration with the difficulties people have in these areas, and after pleas from the students who take my workshops, I've written books about everything from how to deal with difficult people to putting humor and good storytelling into speeches and presentations, to the effective use of PowerPoint. Yes, I even have a class and a book with the same title, *Death by PowerPoint: How to Avoid Killing Your Presentation and Sucking the Life Out of Your Audience.* It is full of simple, yet sensible rules.

As I stress in my PowerPoint primer, I just want the technology you're using to work for you, not against you.

***

Let me tell you what else I think qualifies me to present the ideas in the following chapters. I have some history! I was a member of the workforce long before the Internet was invented. In fact, I date back to the pre-computer days. I was once an IBM Selectric gal, and there was a time I didn't even have a cell phone. So I speak from some experience, know-how and wisdom since I have been on the sidelines watching technology evolve in the workplace. I have witnessed how necessary it is—but I have also taken note of how much it can also become a detriment. In view of the latter, and to vent my frustration, I have even taken pot-shots, lampooning technology, chipping away at it satirically as a sketch comedy writer. (Once I even staged a skit about a couple trying to complete their wedding vows, only to be constantly interrupted by their PDAs and cell phones. When the minister finally storms off they don't even notice. She's verifying the color and style of those shoes she ordered from Nordstrom, while he's giving some final instructions to close a real estate deal by the end of the day.) Fess up. Does this exaggerated scenario sound remotely familiar?

Though I have poked jabs at technology, I like to think that I have been a good sport, evolving right along with it through its many incarnations and advancements, all the while extolling its virtues and embracing its many benefits. I've even tried not to be too critical of its downside. The truth is, I myself am a "user." I am addicted to technology and to email! We all are, I suppose. That's not the point. The point is this: if we're going to shoot off emails for the better part of the day, let's get some decorum going. Let's endear people to us, not alienate them. What do I mean by that? Well, when people start using email for firing people, ending business relationships, canceling contracts, quitting their jobs, giving performance reviews, breaking the news about being way over budget, in other words, communicating vital information in such an impersonal way, enough is enough. We need a manual—an email etiquette playbook.

So what else qualifies me to provide one? I also have substantial background in acting, producing and directing improvisational comedy. I use its techniques and theories to get my lessons across enjoyably in my classes. People love to learn what I teach because of the way I teach it—the way I *communicate* the improv "rules" to them. Believe it or not, appropriate and good improv has a set of manners that goes along with it, too. There is an improv code, and without putting it into play, those of us who perform it would crash and burn. Think about it: Much of our email communication is passed back and forth in an improvisational manner, isn't it? Some of what I will share with you later has to do with how improv actors function while communicating back and forth on stage. You will see how many of their "rules" aptly apply to trading emails effectively.

***

Through all of ExecuProv's workshops, we constantly reinforce one central theme: "Your job is to make the human connection." For in the end, I caution my students—whether working with the big or little "cheeses"—good business is about good relationships. If you cannot connect, you cannot establish, build and maintain rapport. No rapport, no relationship. No relationship, no sale. And, we are all selling something: a service, a product, a philosophy, an idea. But here's the irony: email has created a dynamic by which people can distance themselves from one another. If not used appropriately, email can actually weaken relationships. It can also isolate us. The less we connect with others the more remote and distanced from humanity we become. Email has exacerbated this dilemma. For some, getting caught in this quagmire is a gradual process. For others, it happens the moment they sign up with an email provider.

***

You may be one of the readers who will argue that email actually strengthens relationships, making certain ones possible that would not otherwise exist. And you may also argue that email keeps people more constantly in touch. To some extent that's true. But *how* people are communicating in the process is what disturbs me—e.g. convoluted messaging, poorly crafted style, curt, blunt directives, and no focus on how their message will be received or perceived. These are only some of the issues with email communication of which this book seeks to make readers aware. Sadly, I don't believe email has made for better business relationships at all. My findings have revealed the opposite. I think email has actually hampered and dismantled many of our workplace relationships, both internally and externally. Because so many people spend a good part of their work day facing a computer screen now, I also think we are becoming more detached, thus socially inept. Once again, when we separate ourselves from humanity on a regular basis, it makes it doubly hard to make and keep meaningful connections. I have some students who tell me that they communicate 90 percent of the time by email; only 10 percent of the time do they have verbal dialogue with others. I find that frightening. That said, don't misunderstand me. I do agree that email can be a blessing. It has been for me, too. I just want to point out how it can also be a curse, and how we can work to avoid that.

So, the purpose of this book is not unlike the missions of my other books and the corresponding classes, to help people use their chosen communication tools more effectively. If the way we normally use email is creating communication anarchy and negatively impacting relationships, and if we all want to show respect and be respected when using email, then we need to establish some simple guidelines with the focal point on downright good manners!

The etiquette in this book works. Its theories have been proven through experience in my own professional relationships, and the simple manners I'm recommending are effective, according to my students. They say that by adhering to the *Bliss or "Diss" Connection* guidelines they have maximized their personal and business relationships through email. They have also come face-to-face with where they may be falling short in the email department. For one student it was a simple spellcheck adjustment. Another realized she talked in circles, confusing her recipient. Another was lax in responding and yet another always said things he later regretted.

If you are unable to attend my one-day *Bliss or "Diss" Connection* email class, this book is the next best thing. Here is what the book covers and what my rules address:

- A personal assessment of how you use email
- A hard look at the pros and cons of email communication
- Why you (and others) love it and hate it
- When to email your communication and when to verbalize it—human to human
- The length, style and format for different types of email communications
- The most common mistakes email users make
- How to compose emails that hit the mark
- A close personal examination of whether your emails are naughty or nice

- How email makes you feel—both good and bad—and why
- What's next in technology

***

Though I do not know you, I am willing to bet that you are making major email *faux pas* in the course of your business day and that you are occasionally, if not always, shortchanging your relationships through the use of email. I am also willing to wager that you have no idea how your emails are being received and perceived by others, nor do you always consciously realize how incoming ones are affecting you. You may also be oblivious as to what is appropriate and what is not when using email for business purposes. I know people who do not even know they are breaking the law at times with their emails! But let's forget the legal aspects. This book is about good manners and effective communication through this use of technology. Its thrust is to make sure email works to your benefit, not your detriment.

One of the problems most of us have is that we multitask our way through every business day. As such, we find it hard to focus on just one thing at a time. So, here's your first assignment. Shut off your BlackBerry (or whatever other handheld device you may own) or swing around in that office chair and turn your back to your computer. Perhaps, consider shutting it down completely. Now flip off that cell phone, and put your attention on the lessons in this book.

Yes, I know, "you've got mail," but it can wait. Don't you want to use more effective tools and better manners when creating or responding to it? I thought so. Now, turn the page and let's get started.

"The board has been waiting since Tuesday, Meyers. What excuse should I use today?"

Chapter One

BLISS OR "DISS?"
Heavenly communication or hell to pay.

I thought I'd died and gone to heaven the day I sent my first email. Wow! What a blast. And it was, almost literally. I just typed some words, pushed a button and launched that message right into cyberspace. I dubbed myself the P.R. Astronaut! To add to my euphoria, I kept hearing that familiar voice—the slightly enthusiastic butler-gentleman who eagerly informed me, "You've got mail." "Well, thank you," I caught myself saying more than once out loud, to no one in particular because I was usually in my office all alone. For a long time the email volley was a delight. I'd send an email. I'd get one in return. I'd send one, I'd get one, I'd send one, I'd get one…. I enjoyed every suspenseful click of the mouse just to see who the email was from and what it said. I was almost manic about responding. I couldn't wait to answer!

THE BLISS CONNECTION?

Ah yes, email: almost paradise! What bliss!
That is, until I realized I had become an addict.

I confess, it wasn't long before I couldn't wait to get to work every day to shoot up some AOL. I no longer have to make calls, I told myself. I can back off from the tedious letters. I can just zip through the day, producing twice as much work.

Unfortunately, for me email was becoming my heroin of communication. Soon, I couldn't use it just sometimes. In short order, I came to depend on it regularly.

And then along came Instant Messaging, Text Messaging! You practically had to hold me back with the advent of the BlackBerry. I thought I was going to pass out from sheer delight the first time my thumbs hit the keypad. Whoever dubbed it "CrackBerry" was right on the money. The problem with it though is that, like crack, the PDA high is short-lived between hits. The craving for "sending and receiving" escalates.

I have heard of people bolting out of the middle of a movie, telling the person with whom they came in that they just *had* to get some popcorn. But it was a lie. I know people (and you probably do, too) who excuse themselves with a sense of urgency to use the bathroom. They're lying as well. I know people who have had fender benders while retrieving messages, interrupted their lovemaking, practically gotten arrested in mid-flight, and many others who have completely alienated their significant others and/or children because they were "using." But what are we to do? We're hooked, especially those of us in Corporate America.

THINK AGAIN

I don't think about things as much as I used to. I'm too busy checking my PDA. I don't converse as much as I once did. I'm too busy "sending and receiving." I don't leave the office behind anymore. I can't. It's just too tempting to take it with me—and I do, wherever I go.

Like all good things done in excess though, there is

always a price to pay. I love chocolate, but it doesn't look all that great on my thighs and butt. Maybe you like Jack Daniels, but consuming it regularly could cause you liver disease or get you a DUI. Are you one of those who like an exhilarating hand of blackjack? Eventually, it can cost you your life's savings, right? Is a weekly trip to the mall cutting into your grocery budget? What about bench-pressing more pounds than you did yesterday? That can lead to anything from a torn muscle to a heart attack. As we all know, when we're thinking rationally, any habitual behavior, if overdone, can produce a downside. Addictions always do. But most addicts cannot be rational when it comes to what they're hooked on. They just get a craving to have what they have to have when they have to have it. So, yes, when we overdo we become addicts.

Once addicts, we are clearly headed for trouble.

When you consider that most of us in the workplace spend the majority of our time on the job, "using" technology to get the job done.... Well, you do the math.

But how are we in Corporate America supposed to function without our technological fix, more specifically, without relying heavily on our email communication? We can't now, it's impossible. But as I said in the Introduction to this book, we can set some boundaries and rules. If not, like other hit-the-skids addicts, we're going to lose it. (I keep wondering if soon someone will come out with a patch like they did for nicotine users. Perhaps someone will make a killing with PDA rehab centers or perhaps some psychiatrist will specialize in "email distress disorder.")

LOSE IT IF YOU USE IT?

When I say lose it, I'm not talking about your mind. I'm talking about your human connections. I'm talking about keeping your relationships intact. If you have any question whatsoever about whether any one of your relationships is suffering because of your email addiction, then it's time to start paying attention to the *Bliss or "Diss"* rulebook. Without meaningful relationships, we're in real trouble.

Before I lay out my first set of rules, let me provide some clarity about the word "bliss" as I define it in relation to email. Bliss is a state of delight, a sense of ecstasy, pleasure, harmony; in short, heaven. I'm sure I speak for many business professionals when I say that the accessibility of email has produced a good deal of instant gratification and pleasure. It's fast, it's smooth, it's easy. However, the opposite of bliss is misery and I have heard about plenty of that, too; mainly from my students who have taken my email course and shared their email nightmares, the most common of which is the "diss" connection.

THE "DISS" CONNECTION?

What is the meaning of "diss" connection in my book, both literally and figuratively? For starters, to be "dissed" is to be discarded, dismissed, discounted. The rappers tell us the term is an abbreviation for the word "disrespect" —not showing it to another person. In the end, it denotes some type of rejection or putdown. So when you show disinterest (in someone's email communication to you), or genuine disrespect (you chose not to answer an email within a reasonable period of time or ever!) or you displease (annoy or offend someone with an email), you're well within what Snoop Dogg, 50 Cent, Eminem and the others call the "diss" department.

When I teach my *Bliss or "Diss"* email workshops, I put the "diss" focus on the word "<u>dis</u>connection." The opposite of "involvement." *Webster's Dictionary* says that disconnection is "a separation of things (or people) that (who) were formerly linked." So when we "diss" in the email world, we typically disengage, disenfranchise, disjoin, disaffiliate and disassociate. More importantly, when we disconnect we detach. With email, it is oh so easy to blow someone off, to decide not to communicate with them at all, or to answer them on your timetable, your terms. These behaviors foster separation, detachment and a lack of involvement. It is hurtful to diss someone and also painful to be on the receiving end. Every email user I know has walked in both shoes. Each has been the Dissor or the Dissee.

There is another word that fits within the "diss" category: that word is "distance." That's a big word to ponder when you're sizing up where you stand in relation to others and email. Think about it. If your emails are creating some form of separation—some distance—between you and the others in your business world, isn't it time to rethink your approach to email communications? And how about diplomatically calling others on their email shortcomings? Isn't it about time to clear the air? After all, communication is supposed to close the gap, bring people together, and help us to *connect*.

The opening remarks in every class I teach in each one of the ExecuProv workshops includes an emphasis on making the human connection. I tell my students that is their most important job on the job, to connect with others, whatever it takes.

TESTING, ONE, TWO, THREE...

For starters, take this short quiz to gain some insight into how hooked you are (blissed out) on email and how you may be "dissing" people without meaning to:

1. I use email every day: Yes_____No_____

2. I only use email at the office: Yes_____No_____

3. I check email during every waking hour:
   Yes_____No_____

4. _____% of my communication with others is done through email

5. I check emails all weekend: Yes_____No_____

6. I send emails to others within my office:
   Yes_____No_____

7. I check emails during meetings: Yes_____No_____

8. I feel compelled to answer emails as soon as I read them: Yes_____No_____

9. I check email while on vacation: Yes_____No_____

10. I sometimes lie in order to find a way to check my email when I know I'm not supposed to:
    Yes_____No_____

11. I check email while I'm talking on the phone to others: Yes_____No_____

12. I prefer sending an email rather than making a phone call: Yes_____No_____

13. I prefer sending an email rather than meeting someone in person: Yes_____No_____

14. I answer emails when I feel like it: Yes_____No___

AND THE ANSWER IS…

If you answered yes to questions 1, 3, 5, 6, 7, 8, 9, 10, 11, 12 and 13 you clearly have email "issues." If you answered no to question number 2, your issues are critical. Also, if you responded to number 4 with more than 40 percent, you have work to do!

If, on the other hand, you said yes to number 2 and no to at least half of the items to the questions, maybe you're using email in moderation. That's what you want to aim for.

Still, if you answered yes to most questions, then it's time to do a reality check because you're bliss may just turn to diss over time. However, if you spend more time communicating in person or by phone, I applaud you. I believe we need more of that kind of interaction. Face-to-face or voice-to-voice communication is clearly what the business world (and humanity) is begging for. The only way we can get back to some middle ground in regard to better and more effective communication is through a mixture of email and live dialogue (leaving a voice mail does not count). Yep, I believe we're leaning far too heavily on technology to do the talking for us. If we're going to use email, we need to utilize it in a way that connects, not *disconnects* us from others.

And, we have to find a way to use it in moderation.

Ironic, isn't it? The very tool that is designed to keep us so connected (and it can if used appropriately) is the very tool that often alienates us.

That revelation brings me to the most important lesson in this chapter, determining whether email for you is a bliss or a diss experience. If, according to the quiz, you are heavily addicted to email as a communication means, you're an over-blisser and I promise you you're going to crash one day. Now, if you're lucky, you may just get fed up with the lack of luster in your relationships and alter your email habit all by yourself. Or maybe it will take an intervention or wakeup call. This happened to a friend of mine who told me his secretary threatened to quit because she had chronicled their personal communication for a month and had discovered that they spoke an average of only ten minutes each day, yet he emailed her for more than three hours daily to direct her workload. "She said she was lonely," he told me. "She felt like she was working for a computer, not a person." It was a sobering experience for my friend. He got clean, with his communication. He now says he's done dissing. He gets up out of his chair and walks across the hallway to communicate with her or calls her on the intercom to discuss the day's work activities. Are *you* an over-disser, an over-blisser or both? It's important that you identify where you fall on the bliss/diss scale because only then can you take the rules that apply to you and put them into play.

MY MOTHER ALWAYS TOLD ME...

Some of my *Bliss or "Diss"* fundamental tenets are based upon those simple yet wonderful admonishments my mother used to give me: always be polite and courteous. Pay attention. Be nice. Play fair. And, of course, the rule of all rules: do unto others as you would have them do unto you. Can you recall others from your mom? Good, because you may want to begin to incorporate them into your daily email routine. Once you do, the outcome will probably astound you. For homework, I ask my classes to spend one day just focusing on the notion of "courtesy." So far, every single one of them has reported that they have had some type of "connection breakthrough" with a business associate with whom they had been feeling some distance or lack of rapport because of this shift in their approach to handling their email communications.

Now, write down a few of the things *your* mother always told you to help you reconsider your approach to future email communications. I've allowed a list for ten, but don't stop there. Perhaps you have others. Go ahead, fill in the blanks:

1. _____

2. _____

3. _____

4. _____

5. _____

6. _____

7. _____

8. _____

9. _____

10. _____

Now, choose your favorite one, put in on a Post-it and stick it to the bottom of your computer screen. It will serve as a constant inspiration to develop a better email attitude.

I wrap my entire concept for the *Bliss or "Diss"* rulebook around the admonishment to "Do unto others…" because it snaps me out of my self-centered approach of what works for me. When using email, I believe we all need to think of how we would like to be treated and treat others accordingly. Why is that so hard to do? I believe it's because we're all in such a hurry to get more done in the course of a workday that we don't stop long enough to take the time it requires to demonstrate a little more humanity. Perhaps this is because we have sequestered ourselves, sometimes for hours, in a workspace with a computer instead of another human being.

UP CLOSE AND PERSONAL

Something I want you to always remember about the basics of email etiquette is that your email communication should reflect the same manners you put into play when dealing with someone *in person*. For example, if you were in the company of an individual and they said something to you, would you simply ignore them? No. You'd offer a reply. How many times though have you ignored a non-spam email because you didn't have time to answer, you weren't very interested in the person who sent it, just didn't want to deal with the issue they presented, were just too lazy to respond or simply wanted to avoid a confrontation?

As I keep saying, email makes it easy to blow off someone.

Also, how many times have you been in such a hurry that you shot off an email with a curt and blunt missive without putting some human touch to it like, "Have a great day," "It's good to be in touch again," or "Let's talk soon" in the text? If you're guilty of this, you may be one of those users who doesn't realize your emails are being taken the wrong way or misinterpreted. When you rush and don't reread and edit your email, or you forego the idea of being somewhat personable, I promise you will inadvertently alienate others.

NOW READ THIS!

Don't forget that the email recipient can't see or hear you, they can only *read* you! Which brings me to my next point: when there is no tone of voice, it's hard to get the message across. That means each of us has to work harder to communicate our true intent. When you're in someone's presence, you have the benefit of expressing yourself through inflection, mood, energy and body language. Those communication skills don't translate well, if at all, through most emails. It is close to impossible to demonstrate personality in emails unless you've learned to be a good writer who knows how to create winning copy. Though I am a copywriter, I'm guessing that 90 percent of Corporate Americans are not. (I get their emails!) I'm reminded of what it is like to be an actor who picks up a script to read it cold. Any good actor can change the entire intent of the dialogue by reading the same words, by intoning or phrasing them differently. In my business improv classes we study how to use our emotions to strengthen communication techniques and get our points across. We give each student the same set of ten sentences, along with two pages of emotions (180 all together). Then we ask them to read each sentence in each of the 180 different moods. If the sentence "I've got a business meeting scheduled this morning" is intoned 180 different ways, can you imagine the possible variations? It is remarkable to note how many distinctive meanings can be expressed. When you are in someone's presence, the intent of your words is often fairly clear (unless your communication is riddled with subtext, which I will address in a later chapter). So, be mindful of making your meaning clear and unmistakable. Know that words in your emails can be interpreted differently depending on who's receiving them. Also, keep in mind that when you're talking to someone in person, you have the benefit of using facial animation and body language to further express your messages. No one can see you in email or on the phone so it's imperative that you convey a tone. As I said, they read only words. Therefore, you must find ways to translate feelings along with thought. Sorry, but those little symbols (emoticons) like ☺ and LOL don't have the same punch and impact as the spoken word. Again, consider how you currently treat people with whom you interface. Do they get the message clearly, the intent behind your words? Do you convey your information in such a way that you create a connection with others rather than creating distance? Answering these questions will guide you as you choose new ways to approach the way in which you handle your future email communications.

A LITTLE ETIQUETTE GOES A LONG WAY

With those considerations in mind, let me roll out my first set of fundamental etiquette guidelines when using email. These are simple yet effective primers:

1. **SEND NOW—or send later, but don't send all of the time.** If you're a true email addict you will be both an over-blisser and an over-

disser. It's moderation you're after. Otherwise, chronic and obsessive use of email will cut off a good many of your human connections.

2. **KEEP AS NEW—every email business relationship that you have made and wish to nurture.** All business relationships should be treated like gold, so don't let your email show a gradual sense of "diss"interest. Treat people with the same courtesy that you did when you first met or emailed them (and like you would if you were in their presence). Don't get lazy just because you've established familiarity with someone.

3. **REPLY—to every email within 24 hours unless it is spam.** Leaving people hanging in cyberspace is rude. If you were in someone's presence and they said something to you, would you just stand there silent for hours or days? I didn't think so. Email requires responses in a timely manner. Don't forget the Golden Rule!

4. **SUBJECT—line of your emails should have a specific point.** What's the main point of your email? State it. Make your messages incisive and clear. No one wants to take a read around the block trying to get to the heart of your message. And you don't want your message misinterpreted, so while being exact, be careful not to accidentally diss in the process. All your emails should reflect the same warmth and cordiality you would offer if you were speaking to that person on the street, on the phone or in their office. Use words that will keep the message short and sweet, but warm and personable, too.

5. <u>**DELETE—anything you would never want repeated, forwarded on to someone else or want to see in print (e.g. the newspaper)**</u>. Oft times we are impulsive and say things we shouldn't say in email—things we later come to regret. In contentious or delicate communication situations, this is particularly so. Thinking before you type is also important for legal reasons. In business, emails can be used against you. Pause and reread your email. Edit it if you have to. You never want to suffer "email remorse."

6. <u>**SEARCH MAIL—for any emotional undercurrent from the sender**</u>. Maybe the person communicating with you is trying to appeal to you for help or encouragement or support without really saying so. Address the hidden meanings when replying so you can genuinely show your wish to connect, but do so in a diplomatic, polite, appropriate, professional and cordial way, just as you probably would if you encountered this fellow colleague in your office, on the phone or inside the company cafeteria.

7. <u>**SAVE—any relationship you think or feel is being compromised because of poor email communication between the two of you**</u>. When in doubt, PICK UP THE PHONE! Many a customer has been lost because the message sent was taken the wrong way. Don't just ignore (diss) the person, do something. This includes the co-worker down the hall. Do whatever you can to get the relationship back on track.

8. **REPLY ALL—the time, but not necessarily by email.** For every three emails you send, make one personal contact either by phone or in person. That tells someone she/he matters. It also allows you the opportunity to bond more meaningfully. This rule includes communication with associates, colleagues, fellow workers, clients and customers. Everyone is important.

9. **MAIL OPTIONS—are at your fingertips and there are many choices when it comes to composing or responding to emails.** Get creative. Stay fresh. No one email should ever be the same, canned and pat. Approach each email with this question: What will it take to maximize the human connection? Don't always use the same opener or the same closer. That tells the receiver (if they are a regular communicator with you) that you have no interest in being current, original or creative in your communication with them. It makes them think you lump them in with everyone else with whom you communicate every day. If your email does not include something specific about them, redo it. Surprise them. Brighten their day. Bliss them!

10. **PRINT—out any emails you may need for record keeping.** Don't chance that you will keep emails in your saved mail on your computer. Servers crash, files become corrupt and computer files often mysteriously disappear. We all need certain records tucked away in safe places. It is important to most of us in business to be able to go back and document our communication or reread an email for clarity. Memories fade away and

so do emails. Don't take a chance. Print out hard copies and lock them away in a fireproof filing cabinet.

11. **ATTACH — some personality to your emails.** Compose them in such a way that your messages offer energy, good intent and a pleasing tone. Your voice needs to come through in your emails. Think personality. Think connection. Think about the recipient hearing you, really reading *you*, not just your words.

12. **EDIT — all your emails for proper grammar, punctuation and spelling.** Nothing discredits you faster than sloppy email. Yes, you have spellcheck, I know, but not everyone hooks it up. Sometimes a word is spelled properly but misused. Proofread. Nothing says, "I'm not a business professional," faster or more loudly than poor composition or writing skills.

13. **MANAGE MAIL — in such a way that it comes across as if you were speaking.** Many emails are written like formal letters. Formality does not work in email. Your email communication should sound as though you are *talking* to another person. Conversing. Remember that you already have to fight the separation and distance factor that happens from computer to computer.

14. **REQUEST RETURN RECEIPT — for very important emails.** Or, ask the recipient for confirmation of your email to them. It is not uncommon for an email to float away in cyberspace. Ask your recipient to let you know they have received your message even

if they can't answer you immediately. I've seen more people have misunderstandings, fallings out and hurt feelings because of unanswered emails, only to find out later that the intended never received the piece of communication in the first place.

These are just a few of the rules I am suggesting to get you started. What about the rules for choosing between whether you should email, call or communicate with someone in person? What about the proper length of emails: short or long? How can you really tell if your email communication is naughty or nice? Well, there are more rules that address those email issues, too. For now, let's move ahead to the next chapter for a look at what other email "users" have to say about what they love and hate about email. Some responses you'll relate to instantly, others may be real eye-openers for you! This chapter will also get you thinking about what *you* like and dislike about email communication.

Chapter Two

LOVE OR HATE?
I adore it, I can't stand it.

When it comes to email I can only say that I haven't had this much ambivalence about anything since my last marriage. There were days when I wanted to run my head (or his) through a wall and other days when I was completely and utterly charmed and enamored of him. Just like that man, email can inspire a wild gamut of emotions in me. There are days when my inbox makes me want to toss my computer out the window out of sheer frustration (and I would if I thought my insurance would cover it), and other days when I just absolutely adore the convenience of what email provides me.

I know I'm not alone.

Everyone I queried about what they liked and disliked about email said the same thing. They loved it and they hated it, too. However, when asked if they would be willing to discontinue their relationship with it, they all said no.

CHRONIC COMPLAINING

I hate it that people can just ignore me if they don't want to communicate with me—they can just leave me hanging

29

in cyberspace—and I also despise the fact that it takes me three times longer to type a message than to communicate it over the phone or in person. I don't like the time it takes me to edit my messages (because most writing requires a little of that), and I can't stand getting all the spam, the jokes I don't have time to read and the sales pitches that clutter my screen. I especially hate the fact that one of my favorite ExecuProv students' email system keeps blocking my mail because my address (<u>cheriekerr@aol.com</u>) suggests to his server that I am some sort of porn star who wants to have Internet sex with him or something. So now, every time I want to communicate with him, I have to call him and that seems to annoy him. He says he would rather I email him. That's when I just want to ram my head straight through the screen on my Dell desktop. My biggest pet peeve is when I email someone to remind them they haven't answered the question in my previous email. I would rather someone tell me to go straight to hell than leave me wondering.

I'm ambivalent with it all, because the truth is, I don't think I could get through one single day now without email. As a communications skills expert, it is the tool I use to do a good part of my job. Just ask me how fast I changed my tune from bitching and moaning to desperation the day my DSL line went down. I found myself groveling beneath the lower row of my keyboard, knowing I would give anything for just one more email. Talk about feeling completely isolated and alone and at the mercy of the god of email!

Once you've had email, there's no letting go. You just have to love hating it and hate the fact that you love it so much.

As I mentioned earlier in the book, we're all addicts, email junkies. Since I don't plan to let go of my habit, the next best thing is for me to find ways to minimize what I hate about it and savor the good stuff. How about you?

SOMEBODY, ANYBODY, HELP ME!

To help me gain a better understanding of where the

real problems lie in the love/hate department with email and what we all might do about it, I asked a cross section of strangers, clients, friends and family what they liked and disliked about email. It was both surprising and reassuring to learn that most of us were pretty much on the same page. There were some differences, however, between personal likes and dislikes.

I have presented a number of verbatim responses on the following pages for your satisfaction and edification. Maybe many of these comments will resonate with you, while others will not. That's the basic problem in email communication as I see it: as we go about our business day, it's apparent that we don't all agree about what constitutes email protocol. That's why we hit the wall with each other (and often bungle our relationships). As I mentioned in the Introduction, if there were no rules of the road, we could do the same thing driving cars—hit walls and injure other people. But fortunately, the Department of Transportation has laid out some very specific rules and, like them or not, we go by them in order to avoid accidents. Likewise, we must observe some "driving protocols" when we launch our emails out onto the Internet highway.

That's why we need reasonable rules for email—a *Department of Email Handbook*! There are just too many email mishaps.

SURVEY SAYS

I asked all of my volunteers two questions: "What do you like about email?" and "What do you dislike about email?" See if you can relate to any of their responses.

What I like about email:
"It's great when you have a job like I do, where you're on the phone all day. It allows me to stay in touch with more than one person at the same time."

What I dislike about email:

"The only bad thing about email is that sometimes you don't always get them. Companies have spam systems and sometimes emails get lost in the abyss of cyberspace. It's always a good idea to follow up (especially if you don't get a response from someone!)."

Annie Scranton
Executive Producer
Geraldo at Large
New York, New York

***

What I like about email:

"It's less intrusive than a phone call, as I can respond at my convenience, not at someone else's convenience."

What I dislike about email:

"Sarcasm doesn't work!"

Diane K. Danielson
CEO, downtownwomensclub.com
Cohasset, Massachusetts

***

What I like about email:

"You can communicate quickly with the recipient. You can have your say and get your message to the person faster than you can with snail mail. This way the message reaches the person faster and you can close your business arrangements quicker. An example is when I am looking to obtain new clients. I email them my resume and samples before I mail it to them. I haven't touched a stamp in a long time."

What I dislike about email:

"The way you word things and the failure of technology to deliver it. You can communicate your message all you want, but if you

do not use proper words, the person the message was intended for may get the wrong idea from the way you expressed it and may have hurt feelings. Then that person will respond, blasting you for your previous email, not realizing your comments were not meant to be taken that way. The other factor is when you've finished your email and try to send it, but a technical problem occurs at either your end or your ISP's end. That is exasperating, to say the least."

Harry Husted
Full-time Writer/Author/Researcher
Bronx, New York

***

What I like about email:
"Easy and quick. I can type fast and it is easier than leaving a voicemail."

What I dislike about email:
"Very impersonal and unemotional. This can cause miscommunication, and stress business relationships. There is no 100 percent guarantee that the recipient received the email. Servers can crash, email can go into the spam box, etc. There are responsiveness expectation gaps, people have very different concepts of what constitutes a timely manner to respond to email. Some people only check email every few days and prefer the telephone."

Seth Hishmeh
Co-founder/COO
USAS Technologies, LLC (IT Technologies)
U.S., India and China

***

What I like about email:
"It's better than a fax communication because often words from a fax can get cut off. Also, I can store photos and contracts and other important documents in an archive on my computer for

safekeeping and to email to others. In my work that's important; in that respect, I find email a more efficient way of doing business."

What I dislike about email:
"I hate it when people forward your email address without permission or put you on a bulk email list or when I receive an email and there is no note in the subject box. I also don't like it when people send more than two or three attachments. I hate junk mail and I don't like receiving a contract when it hasn't been signed and dated prior to sending. I also don't like it when people don't respond to my emails."

Keith Dugger, ATC
Head Athletic Trainer
Colorado Rockies Baseball Club
Denver, CO

***

What I like about email:
"I like how quickly I can communicate with people, how succinct it can be, how it protects me from long conversations I can't end with people. It helps me to think more clearly. It's also a great way to send out mailings to thousands of people who subscribe to my newsletters."

What I dislike about email:
"I dislike how much endless email I get and how some people procrastinate sending you an email, but then want an immediate response from you. I hate how addicted I have become to checking it. How easy it is to make a mistake and send the wrong email to the wrong person. It is also upsetting to receive terse, one-word answers (BlackBerry) or long endless ones."

Mark Goulston, M.D.
Psychiatrist and Author
Los Angeles, CA

35

***

What I like about email:
"It's quick and easy."

What I dislike about email:
"I cannot disconnect from it. Whether I'm in Thailand or in the car, I compulsively check my email. No vacation, no situation keeps me from checking."

Laurie Brown
Author of *TelePrompTer Manual*
Pontiac, Michigan

***

What I like about email:
"You can quickly send an answer to someone."

What I dislike about email:
"You don't see the body language (non-verbal) part of communication. The little LOL notations or smiling faces just don't do it. I'm afraid a great deal of communication gets lost in email."

Elaine Fantile Shimberg
PR Leads
Tampa, FL

***

What I like about email:
"It's a fast way to communicate. I sometimes work late in to the night and I can get a lot done through email."

What I dislike about email:
"I really believe that you can accomplish a lot more with people in a face-to-face meeting than you can trying to get the same job done through back-and-forth emails. There is no question that I can

accomplish my communication goals in half the time in person. This is especially true when dealing with a handful of people. By the time you get around to everyone, it could take days! What I also dislike about email is that you have to be very careful how you say things. People often take you the wrong way."

Drake Doremus
Film Director/Writer
Los Angeles, CA

***

What I like about email:
"The ability to be able to communicate to a large group of people instantly and having the ability to get documented feedback within a short period of time."

What I dislike about email:
"Many abuses. First, being copied from a list in a person's address book when the communication is not something I need to receive. Second, the folks that hit the 'reply all' when the response was really intended only for the original sender. Third, the power to be able to forward confidential information to the whole world and, lastly, the fact that many people hide behind email. These addicted types come into their offices and communicate without actually talking to anybody for hours at a time. A negotiation that should be handled by phone, or better yet face-to-face, becomes diluted with 20 email responses. The negotiation problem could have been resolved more efficiently through an interactive conversation and, in most cases, the participants would leave feeling better about the outcome."

Richard Bartolic
American Pacific Trucking and
President, California Trucking Association
Chino, CA

***

COMMON GROUNDS

Notice any common ground among those I interviewed? Me too! It seems that what most people like about email is that it's quick, easy and efficient. What I heard in the dislike department was one complaint after another about messages that can be misconstrued, overstated, unclear—and then, of course, I also heard a recurring theme of feeling angry, hurt or disappointed at being "dissed."

The latter is one of the big problems with email.

Overall, though, I felt that people had the same basic needs and wants in terms of email: they all wanted to communicate in a faster way, they didn't want to be bogged down with clutter, and also they wanted to be understood by their recipients and be treated decently by them.

As I pored through my responses, I was greatly relieved to see that I was not alone in my addiction, nor was I an outsider about what I liked and disliked about email. The survey results did much to bolster my resolve in wanting to come up with a code to live by in the email world.

IRRECONCILABLE DIFFERENCES

In Chapter One, I suggested a broad set of rules, all of which I truly believe will work and which I think should be put into the *Department of Email Handbook*. Now I'd like to offer a few additional guidelines—ones I have field-tested with great success. What else might I have up my email sleeve? Well, believe it or not, my next set of rules is adopted from the same performance handbook used by the improvisational comedy player—the one he or she uses to communicate on stage.

You might immediately argue that when these people are on stage they are communicating face-to-face and live. You're right, but interestingly, you can take their same set of "in-person" rules and easily apply them to email. They still work. In fact, they work well because each rule focuses on one more effective way to make and keep the human connection. Each strategy fits perfectly in terms of composing and responding to emails.

IN THE BEGINNING

Before we get to them, start with this rhetorical question: isn't communication in our daily business lives mostly improvisational? Of course it is! I rather doubt that any of us walk out the door every day with a script to converse with our coworkers any more than we head for the office with a notebook full of pre-written emails—ones that we'll send off in response to those we are about to receive for the day. How could we? A script for verbal and written communication would probably do us no good because we don't know what the other person will say in response to our "lines." Since that's the case, if communication between all of us on the job is generally improvisational and much of that communication is via email, then why not use what the quick-witted masters of always-say-the-right-thing-at-the-right-time use? Ah yes, if we but follow the improv comedy player's rules—or even a few of them—along with those basic email rules I listed in Chapter One—I don't think we can go wrong. So here I go, letting you in on some of the best-kept secrets in the world of impeccable communication—those of the improv comedy player—because with these skills you can't miss when it comes to making the human connection and strengthening your relationships with others.

TRUST: <u>We always show we can be trusted and automatically trust others until they demonstrate that they cannot be trusted.</u> How many emails have you sent out before you had established a sense of trust between you and the person at the other end of the computer link? Maybe you didn't answer their specific question. Maybe you sent an ambiguous response, or maybe you were curt with them, or they with you. Maybe they used something against you that you said in an email. Email already creates a kind of odd distance between us and the other person, and once you've established a certain pattern—namely, one of distrust or doubt—that is the type of relationship you will perpetuate. You should pay close attention to starting every email relationship with ways to demonstrate you can be trusted, openly showing that you are counting on him/her. Here is a fun homework assignment: Make a list of those business colleagues in and out of the office, with whom you communicate primarily through email. Now, on a scale from one to ten, see how you rank your relationship with him/her in the trust department. If you are totally honest, you may be surprised at your findings.

1. **SERVE AND SUPPORT: <u>This rule means that if I am engaged in a piece of communication with another person, I put the focus on what is it I can do to make the communication work for *him/her*, not me.</u>** With email, I think we isolate ourselves so much that our little work-world tends to revolve around "us," not "them." Ponder how much differently your communication might turn out if you put the weight of your attention on the other guy. Make this a cardinal rule. To put it into play, how about asking your business associates what their preferences and expectations are in the way of email communication? Or, if that seems uncomfortable, how about picking up their cues? Do they seem to indicate they want a quick reply, shorter message, more details? To see if rule #2 works, make this your focus for just one day out of your busy work week. Next, notice the difference in your relationship with your colleagues. Yes, for the improv player, serving and supporting ensures that every piece of communication works. Aren't we all improv players?

2. **REACT AND RESPOND: <u>In the improv player's world, we only react and respond to the last</u>**

thing said or last idea held. Though this rule doesn't have much to do with initiating an email, it has everything to do with answering one. How many times have you answered someone's email with a message *you* wanted to send while only partially addressing the content of theirs—or not addressing it at all? Here's a strategy to keep you on track: Though you may be in a hurry, if there is more than one question or issue a person is addressing in his/her email to you, cut and paste each of them as you reply. I have been told by my students that this really helps to clarify each point posed in an email. How much time do you waste clarifying questions or issues to a person to whom you've sent an ambiguous or off-track email?

3. COMMITMENT: **In improv communication we don't have the luxury of picking and choosing which scenes (pieces of communication) we want to respond to with care and those to which we don't. We go at each and every "scene" with equal integrity and commitment.** I don't know about you, but there are days when I just don't feel up to answering 75 emails, so I tend to give more preference to some and less time to others. Still others I blow off entirely. In improv, we don't distinguish between assignments we wish to put energy and interest into and those we don't. Fully committed, we go at every piece of communication with the same complete consideration.

4. GIVE AND TAKE: **We try not to dominate the conversation on stage, nor do we "lay out," a term used to describe those taking a passive, non-responsive position.** We give a little and take a little. We work at getting a nice dance of back and forth, never hogging the communication

and never holding back. Examine which side of the fence you sit on with regard to "Give and Take." If you tend to push other people around with your email, back off. If you make the email communicator do all the work, then step up and do your part to keep email dialogue at parity. If you want to get real serious about this rule, spend just one day assessing where you stand in the give-and-take department. Are you always dominating or always retreating? Could you use a little balance?

5. **DIVISION OF REPSONSIBILITY:** <u>Translated in improv-speak, this means each of us takes our proportionate share in making communication work</u>. If there are four of us on stage, each one of us takes a 25 percent role in moving the communication along. Since (usually) there are two of us doing the email "scene," that means that you and the other person are both 50 percent responsible to make the communication work.

6. **ATTENDING TO:** <u>We always pay attention to whomever is speaking.</u> It's just good manners, yes, but in the improv world it also precludes us from stepping on one another's lines. Though improv players are dealing with one another in person, I believe this rule still applies to the emailer. How much attention do we really pay to what the email sender is saying? Take a day and zoom in on just this one precept. It's a terrific exercise for those times during the day when you are communicating via Instant Messaging.

7. **REFUSAL/DENIAL:** <u>To refuse is to ignore something someone says; to deny is to change or undercut it.</u> If improv players refused or denied one another on stage, their communication would

42

crash. The same goes for us with communication via email. How many times today has someone ignored the issue you addressed in your email? How many times have you bypassed what an emailer sent your way? Also, how many times have you belittled what someone said? How many times have they done this to you? I'll be providing some examples of this in a later chapter.

8. **YES, AND...THEORY: <u>With this rule we go *with* what is said rather than opposing the idea or concept.</u>** We can certainly disagree with someone's point of view, idea or strategy, but we do so after we have "yes...and-ed" the person, basically, "Yes, and I agree with what you are saying, and..." For example, if you tell me that you would rather I not send lengthy emails, but discuss most details in person, I go *with* that idea rather than against it. I don't say things like no, don't, won't, can't, but, shouldn't, etc. All of these are negatives. Instead, I go with a positive approach by saying "Yes, *and* I understand you prefer that I explain the details in person, *and* I'd like to suggest that I can provide them to you just as effectively in an email." I went *with* the idea rather than negating it by saying something like, "No, giving you the details will take forever so forget it." Or, "That's a dumb idea. I'll just email them to you." I took a "yes, and..." approach. I didn't slam up against the request. I attempted to agree with the concept, not the strategy. I showed some consideration.

9. **BEGINNING, MIDDLE AND END: <u>Every improv scene, whether it is three lines or 300 lines, has a beginning, middle and an end.</u>** In improv, we quickly set up the situation then begin to grapple with the issue/problem/need. Once we have done so, we quickly bring the communication

to resolution. If you listened to some of my email survey participants, you heard the complaint about messages being misconstrued or emails not being answered. In other words, people feel "dissed." Go back through just the last hour of your emails. Did the communications you sent have a beginning, middle and end? If not, just for exercise, go back and redo them. You might just begin to understand why some of your "human connections" are not quite connecting.

10. **LISTENING: SURFACE/SUBTEXT: We not only listen to the spoken word—each and every one of them—but we also listen to what lies beneath those words.** This improv comedy rule may well be one of the most important ones to adapt into your email etiquette regime. How many times have you taken, at face value, the words as they are written in an email and not picked up on the non-written cues? I would have to say that we emailers are all guilty of this to some extent. Why? I think it's because we're all in such a hurry, trying to do too much in each given workday hour to really pay attention to where someone is coming from. And there is no tone behind written words. We can't hear these words expressed. Talk about missing the proverbial boat in the human connection department! If you're not already doing so, listen up. By this, I mean increase your attention to the subtexts in your email messages.

11. **ANSWERING THE QUESTION: In the world of improv, we get a set up from the audience—the fodder for the scene we need to work out—and we must address all aspects of that request.** In real life, however, especially with email because it is so common to "diss" and be "dissed," we often blow off the question by not answering it

in part or in total. Great rule, I think. Once again, pull up your "sent" emails for the day. Did you answer the question — provide the information the other person was asking for, or are you guilty of "dissing?"

12. **ECONOMY OF DIALOGUE** — <u>We only say what is absolutely necessary to communicate ideas. The improv player makes every word count.</u> Though I will be spending more time on this later, I want you to pay close attention to whether the emails you're sending are concise and specific, or whether they are convoluted and hard to decipher. This is not to say that we shouldn't show some humanity. One of my biggest complaints — and that of my students and survey takers — is that people are too curt and abrupt in their email messages. This improv rule is more directed toward not overdoing emails by over-explaining everything. A great homework assignment would be to critique those emails you sent just this morning. Are they clear, specific and easy to assimilate? Do they also show some humanity?

13. **CREATING INTO CERTAINTY:** <u>The improv player never communicates in generalities but is always specific and to the point.</u> A scene in improv may only last a minute or two. From the get-go, the performers have to establish the situation so the others on stage will have clarity as to what is going on — what the scene is all about and the direction in which it is heading. In order to do that, the improv actors have to be exact in their messages to one another. If we followed this rule when sending email, we might save precious time rather than going back and forth trying to figure out what the other person meant. We also wouldn't have to waste time explaining ourselves

because the email receiver couldn't understand the intent of our message.

14. **BE HERE NOW:** <u>This is the gospel according to improv—staying in the present moment at all times.</u> I don't know about you, but with the speed of technology I find myself multitasking constantly. What that means is that I'm anywhere but "in the moment" with others much of the time. While I'm sending an email, I'm also talking on the phone and simultaneously acting out a charade-style directive with a staff member. I often find myself jumping ahead or lagging behind, rarely giving my undivided attention to any one thing. In the improv rulebook, this would be considered a mortal sin! If you can hunker down and "be here now" can you imagine how much more on top of your email game you would be? I have come to believe that we very often keep the email ping-pong thing going—wasting valuable time and messing up relationships—because we weren't paying attention in the first place.

I hope you find the improv player's fundamental rules valuable. I know from experience that they work in all communication styles, whether verbal or written. With that in mind, please add these strategies to your email etiquette arsenal along with the rules from Chapter One. By doing so, you'll be well on your way to becoming a well-mannered email user.

While I think we will all remain ambivalent about email to some degree because it is so easy to love and hate, I would like to help you lean more in the "love" direction! In order to get there, let's move on for a rundown of the rules for deciding when it is appropriate to email and when it is proper to call, by phone or in person.

Chapter Three

CALL OR WRITE?
I'll say it—nah, I'll just type it.

I have already confessed to being an email junkie. By now, you probably have, too. Now that we've gotten that out of the way, I want to start this chapter with a hard look at the residual fallout such a habit can produce. Sure it can cause carpal tunnel, eye strain, stiff neck—for PDA users, more calluses on a thumb than Eddie Van Halen gets in ten years of touring—and a host of other related physical ills (not to mention larger rear ends). But what about personality changes? What unwanted characteristics have we acquired as a result of the reach-out-and-touch-by-email phenomenon? I ask because I wish to address such changes before I introduce to you my *Bliss or "Diss"* communication guidelines for when it is appropriate to write it or when you should say it by phone or in person.

Well, for one thing, I think most of us have become lazy.

EASIER WRITTEN THAN SAID

Sloth is not a conscious habit among us email fanatics.

48

Most of us didn't come upon a sense of lassitude overnight. Nope, it crept up on us. Why and how? It's simple. It became so much easier to shoot off an email than to pick up the phone or walk down the hall to someone's office to communicate with them.

Many of my students tell me they think about *saying* whatever it is they wish to communicate, but quickly change their minds and *write* it instead, mainly because it takes much less effort. *Of course*, email is an efficient means of communicating. I keep saying that, but I think most of us have taken it a bit too far. Because we write it rather than say it, in the words of Sofia Coppola, often a lot gets "lost in translation."

For the moment, though, I'm talking about what email has done to change our workplace personalities and how it has created neuroses and phobias. For instance, what about those email neurotics who have to check their BlackBerrys or desktops incessantly? (I bet they make for great pinball wizards.) It's almost become a nervous tic, hasn't it? How about people who experience panic attacks when they suddenly discover at an off-site meeting that they've accidentally left their PDA at the office? Lord have mercy! (It happened to me and I felt like I had left the house without my underwear!)

In addition to becoming lazy, neurotic and phobic, we also have another "personality" issue with which to deal—our social skills. They're really beginning to slip. Many of us sit behind a computer screen emailing all day until we're nearly comatose, so it's a little hard to suddenly behave like the Wal-Mart greeter when someone has the nerve to stop by your office or interrupts your stupor with a phone call. What that means is that many of us (I'm raising my hand) prefer to be alone.

Can you say "hermit?"

Gives a whole new meaning to the term "lockjaw," doesn't it?

Is the art of conversation becoming passé?

Not if I can help it!

BEHAVIOR MODIFICATION

This chapter takes a look at some etiquette that will help us modify or shift our wayward behaviors to a more balanced place. It lays out some additional rules that may prevent us from getting stiff necks, strained eyeballs, and cramped fingers. On the behavioral side, these guidelines for when it is appropriate to email, phone or show up in person are also geared to help us so we won't become even lazier, more neurotic and phobic. They are designed to keep us from regressing further in all the necessary workplace social behaviors. My biggest concern is the emerging trend toward becoming workplace isolationists. That's a huge issue.

EQUAL TIME

I believe we all need to achieve parity—we need to give equal time to all three types of communications at work—written, verbal and up-close-and-personal.

But until we fully embrace email rules and boundaries as a workplace society, I'm convinced emailers will do what they damn well please, and that means we will only add to our psychological maladies. Soon many of us will be heading off to therapy for very different reasons. Instead of feeling bad about something someone has *said* to us, and sharing it with our trusted mental health professional, we will seek help because of what they *wrote* to us. Which makes me worry. Could we be teetering on the brink of a whole new school of psychology: dispensing "email therapy?" Dear me! Perish the thought!

Let's *talk* more, for without a little more conversation and a lot less email, I'm afraid we're going to exchange "human connection" for "loose connection"! After all, as business professionals, shouldn't we be intent on establishing, building and maintaining relationships?

I confess, I myself have been guilty of sitting in a chair all day, not saying much of anything to anyone, just typing away—one email after another. But I believe that's a mistake, a costly one, and I have paid the price more than once. Like the day my P.R. strategy team popped in unexpectedly at the end of the day wanting my opinion on a campaign. It actually took me a minute to pull my head out of my computer, shake out the cobwebs and suit up my social skills before I could engage in conversation with them. Getting the first words out of my mouth was a weird sensation. I think I said something like, "Hey..." Then thankfully, one of them broke the ice with a complete sentence. How about you? Ever feel a distance between you and those with whom you regularly work, and is that gap growing? Ever had a day when, even though you dealt with people by email for eight hours, you were left with the feeling that you never really had contact with anything human? Verbalize—ah yes, we all need to verbalize more.

SHY AWAY

I've never considered myself a shy person, not in the business sense anyway. But my rude awakening came the morning I received a call from a prospective ExecuProv client with whom I had been emailing for a couple of months. He wanted to know about our classes, our fees, our references. I bet we had a good 20 or so emails between us.

I felt we had established a nice relationship, he and I.

Until...one lazy afternoon my assistant told me that Mr. So and So was on the line. Uh oh, not *online*, but *on* the line. I froze. I wasn't ready to *talk*. Not to *him*. I suddenly felt extremely uncomfortable and awkward, as if I were about to open the door to greet a blind date. Actress that I am though, I bravely stepped up and faked it. (Strange when you consider I make speeches before audiences of anywhere from 20 to 2000 people on a regular basis, then I get this phone call and....)

I pretended to be at ease. He was pretending, too, he

later confided, because he also felt uneasy *making* the call. He said he was reluctant to dial, but didn't have the time to play the email dance that day. He needed an answer, pronto. He said he'd resisted for about an hour before he finally dialed me up. I knew how he felt because I, too, have had those days when I have backed away from the dial pad like it was a hot stove, afraid to get too close. I've started to punch those numbers many times, only to swing back over to the computer keyboard to let the email do the talking for me.

There's something wrong with that.

We're writing far too much.

When we get to the point that we begin to lose our communication spontaneity—our ability to act on an impulse to pick up the phone and make a call like we did before the advent of email, when we stammer before we speak, or feel uneasy making or taking a call, then it's time to draw some lines in the communication sand and say, "okay, let's every one of us find some balance in the methods with which we communicate."

LOOK AROUND, AND WITHIN

Before I get to my guidelines and the do's and don'ts for what I think makes for good manners in regards to writing, calling or showing up, I'm going to share a few "student stories." These, I hope, will enable you to reflect on your own decisions regarding when to use email and when to seek verbal and/or human contact.

If you will, look at these stories—and your own experiences—through the window of the *Bliss or "Diss"* rules discussed thus far. As you read these confessions, I think you'll agree that the rules I've suggested could have helped tremendously had these students put them into play.

I asked them one question, "What is the biggest mistake you think you've made thus far on the job by choosing email over making a phone call or paying an in-person visit?" (I use only first names to protect my subjects.) Here is what they had to say:

"I wished my secretary a Happy Birthday by email. She was two offices over from me. She cried. Now I don't even send e-cards to anyone anymore." Damon

"I lost a client because he told me that he didn't feel he knew me that well, and when a competitor came calling (in person) he switched from our accounting firm to his. He cited the "people thing" as his reason. When I emailed him to ask him what he meant by the "people thing," he didn't answer me." Regina

"I sent an email to a new employee. I said some stuff about it being nice that she had joined our team. I was only trying to make her feel welcome when I closed with something about how nice she looked in her outfit. I guess the way I worded it offended her. I don't think it would have sounded that way if I had said it to her face. She tried to tell our boss I was sexually harassing her." Casey

"I don't have good vocabulary, I guess, so when I got this referral I emailed the prospect and told him all about our notary company, that we also provided insurance and stuff like that. He emailed me back, kind of formal, and said he would contact us if he was interested. It really made me feel bad because the guy who referred him to us told me he was going to hire us. My friend (the guy who referred us) later told me I should have called him or taken him out to lunch or something because my personality would have come through. I never did figure out if it was the words I said or because my email wasn't friendly enough. I still feel bad about it." Lindsey

"I had this customer (past tense) who was becoming a good friend, and he called my office one day and left a message for me to call him. I didn't return his call, I emailed him. He got really mad and sent me an email telling me something like. 'If I'm not important enough to call…' I don't know, I can't remember now what all

he said, but we wound up breaking off our relationship—by email. I'm kinda scared to use email anymore. Now I'm calling everybody." Andy

"I got an email from this guy I do work for. I make brochures for him. I was busy, so I didn't answer him for a couple of days. Then it got worse. He started acting snotty in his emails. One day, I didn't answer his question right or whatever, so when he said something negative about how he felt about that in his email, I decided not to email him back. I didn't want the hassle. That was about six months ago and I haven't heard from him since. I don't want to email him but I like to do his work." Cynthia

Every time my students ask what is appropriate and what is not, i.e., when to write and when to say it, I always tell them to view each situation from the perspective of the person with whom they are communicating. I tell them to revisit the improv rules and focus on "Serve and Support." If they can remember that one simple precept, they will undoubtedly keep their business relationships in better shape. For instance, if Cynthia had just picked up the phone and called her client (because she should have sensed she had struck out in the email communication department and needed to contact him personally), she may have salvaged that relationship. She should have considered serving and supporting *his* needs, not her own. That goes for you, too. Always put the focus on the other guy and what will work for him/her. I also ask my students to review all of the other improv rules in Chapter One's etiquette primer in addition to "serve and support" because many of the accompanying rules address this issue.

If you are at all confused about when to write and when to call, here's a great way to get clarity: write down the names of those with whom you communicate on a regular basis at work and take the time (I know that's hard, but worth it) to find out if you are catering to what *they* prefer as you make your connection with them. Not sure? Ask. You may be pleasantly or unpleasantly surprised by their feedback. Even if you think you know what they prefer, ask anyway. Just asking and reviewing their answers may help you fortify your relationships with the people you most need to make your work world go around.

IRON CLAD

In order to build and maintain rapport (trust, like and respect), you must communicate with people in your work environs in a way that keeps your relationships strong and intact. Sometimes we get a feel for what a co-worker or client wants, but other times we simply make assumptions. That's what gets us into trouble. Even without email, that has proven to be a problem: thinking we know what someone is telling us, even though they don't express it directly, and giving their subtext meaning *our* interpretation. In other words, not responding to their point of view because we weren't paying particular attention to where they were coming from. The advent of email, where we reside behind a virtual veil, makes real communication even harder. When you can't see a person's face or view their body language or hear a tone of voice, you tend to go by *your* preferences. It's easy to get lost in your own translation. My suggestion is this: take some time, get off your workplace butt and *communicate.* The following are a few simple questions you might wish to ask those with whom you interact every business day. Ask them either in person, by phone or (ohmygod) in an email:

1. What information do you want emailed to you?
2. What information do you want me to provide you by phone or in person?
3. Do you receive most of your emails on your PDA or on your desktop?
4. I should email you when _____
5. I should call you when _____

6. I should come and see you in person
   when _____

7. I think people fall short in communicating with one
   another in the workplace
   when they _____

8. I define good taste in email
   as _____

9. I define poor taste in email
   as _____

10. I prefer the following ratios of email to phone calls
    to in-person contact. For example, 30 percent email,
    30 percent by phone, 40 percent in person:

    _____ percent by email

    _____ percent by phone

    _____ percent in person

Now that you have some answers, it might be easier for you to compose your own set of workplace guidelines in terms of which form of communication to use in particular situations. Remember one key rule: keep the communication balanced. The simple guideline is this: not too much email and too little human contact, or vice versa, since most business folks use email. If you're not ambitious enough to ask your clients the questions above, take heed of these "don't ever's" and "always do's." I think they will safely guide you in making sound choices when it comes to making a snap decision about whether to write, call or communicate in person:

DON'T EVER:

1. **Send bad news via email.** Either pick up the phone or show up in person to deliver it.

2. **Say anything in an email that you don't want**

broadcast to the world. I touched on this in our first list of rules. We all know that emails can be forwarded to everyone, everywhere, around the entire world in a matter of seconds. Better to say whatever you don't want others to hear to your recipient on the phone or in person.

3. **Criticize or discuss sensitive issues in an email.** Hurting someone's feelings in an email is not only cold, the sting of what you say can penetrate more deeply into a work colleague's psyche and last longer than it would have if you had approached them with some verbal contact—either by phone or in person. Unless you're an extraordinarily diplomatic writer (most emailers are not), there's a good chance you will hit the wall with the recipient. Call or show up in person and say what you have to say with professional kindness.

4. **Email special compliments or congratulations.** Demonstrate how special you think a person's achievements or accomplishments are by picking up the phone or by stopping by to tell them so (even a handwritten note would be a nice touch). I know you may argue with this one, but remember our goal: good manners and strengthening relationships. There is something flat and removed about a pat on the back that comes in an email. If you deliver praise in person, I promise you will make big points with the person on the other end of the compliment. Focus on what value there is in making that verbal human connection. I guarantee your relationship will gain in meaning.

5. **Engage in a shouting match through email.** Pick up the phone or, better yet, ask to meet with the person(s) on the other end to hash things out.

You'll resolve your differences faster that way and probably more positively.

6. **Fire anyone by email**. This is the biggest "diss" and a heartless way to terminate someone's services or position.

ALWAYS DO:

1. **Find out what someone's preferences are regarding your communication with him/her.** Remember to ask the questions I suggested a few paragraphs ago. Especially ask how they like their communication (and email) to be delivered. Restaurant table servers, flight attendants, the guy behind the counter at the cleaners usually ask, "How do you like your (burger, coffee, shirts?)" We should always ask, "How do you like your communication, by email, phone or in person?" "How do you like your email, short, long or in between?"

2. **Give two positives for every negative.** Should you find yourself in a position where you have to send a difficult message and absolutely can't do so by phone or in person, see that the weight of the email message leans toward the positive. This rule helps to soften the blow and leaves the recipient feeling better about the news, whatever it may be.

3. **Let them "see" you in your emails.** If you don't think your written words are showing some personality, go back and edit your message. You want to attach some character to every email so people can feel your presence, not just read your words (a rule I mentioned in Chapter One). If you think your message might not be putting

you across effectively enough, it's time to pick up the phone or show up in person and get the job done.

4. **See the communication need from the other guy's point of view.** What do you think the impact of your message will be on the person with whom you are communicating? Are they bent out of shape by you always emailing? Do they want you to stop by or phone regularly? If your answer is "I don't know," it's time to get more involved in getting to know the people with whom you interact regularly on the job. Maybe Joe Blow wants to talk on the phone more than by email. Maybe he wants some face time. Just because you think *you* should communicate in a particular way, it doesn't mean someone else will want to do the same. Does someone with whom you work want *everything* in email, or could he or she be a more "up-close-and-personal" kind of communicator? You'd better find out.

5. **Sharpen your social skills.** This is especially true if you are a chronic email user and if communicating by email is causing you to isolate yourself from workplace society. I don't want to ever see you lose your edge and spontaneity in the verbal communication department, so put yourself in situations where you are forced to verbalize more. This could mean scheduling regular in-person staff meetings, arranging for a conference call rather than group emails, and stopping by for a quick chat with those people who are within convenient range, in the office or the field. This is particularly important when it comes to customers and clients.

6. <u>**Pick up the phone immediately if you receive an email that conveys anger, hurt or disappointment.**</u> People often make the mistake of following up a disturbing email with another email. Never is there a more propitious time to pick up the phone or make a beeline for the person's office than when you get an email that needs some explanation on your end, some compassion or special attention. Cash in on these instances as opportunities to secure and strengthen your business relationships.

Now that you've taken a close look at the guidelines for either writing it or saying it—and it will differ from person to person—it's time to draw some boundaries. Let's take a look at some etiquette regarding how short or long emails should be. Get ready to pull out some of those emails you have received or written this past week because you will need them to do the homework in Chapter Four.

"It's another Tolstoy-length email from Fenton, so I'll be ordering in dinner."

Chapter Four

SHORT OR LONG?
What's too little, what's enough?

If all your emails read like movie trailers sound ("bold, captivating...a workplace triumph!"), you have work to do. On the other hand, if your emails take as long to get through as a chapter in *War and Peace,* you'd better get to an editing class. While I realize that what is considered proper etiquette for email length is an ongoing debate, I like to think that my suggestions in this chapter will work for you because I've field tested them. I have believed for some time that we are long overdue for establishing some rules as to how short or long emails ought to be. Indeed, we need some uniformity, some decorum.

THE LINE OF DEMARCATION

As we explore what is right and wrong, or best or worst, in terms of format, length, style and so forth, the first point I wish to make is that email has created an entirely new format for written communication. No longer are most business professionals composing messages and information in the formal style of letters that need to be mailed. To me, that's a good thing because those often tend to be long and drawn out, way too "official" and slow for today's corporate tempo. Gee whiz, for the time it takes to write and read letters in today's fast-paced corporate world, you could power down a sandwich and soda for lunch.

I'm glad the letter of yesteryear is all but extinct for other reasons; I think people can make the human connection far more readily, easily and meaningfully by using email because they tend to communicate much more conversationally. Also, when email banter goes back and forth and people are engaging in true communication with one another, good emails can actually enhance the quality of business relationships; that is, if no one engages in the "diss" game or annoys the other person with emails that are either too long or too short.

So, where do you draw the line?

That has been an ongoing point of discussion in all my *Bliss or "Diss"* workshops since they started. In fact, this question is at the heart of one exercise we do in class. Every student is asked to carefully consider what the appropriate length for an email should be. He or she is given emails that are already written and asked to improve upon them—whether than means making them shorter or longer. They are also asked to compose, in teams of two, emails they might send to their bosses, their clients, their co-workers and those they have never met or communicated with before. They are always astounded to compare the before-and-after versions of the pre-written communication they are handed as well as seeing the difference between the third, fourth and fifth drafts of emails they originally composed. They come to realize that most emails are either one or the other: too long or too short. (I will present some before-and-after examples later on in this chapter.)

INCOMING, WATCH OUT

One basic rule of thumb is I give my students is this: if an incoming email is not a press release, a legal brief or several pages of the company handbook (which are usually sent in attachments anyway), but simply a standard message or query, it should not take more than 10 to 20 seconds to read. If it takes more time than that, it's probably too long. The Corporate Worker Bee doesn't have the same attention span he/she once had. Conversely, if the communiqué is something that looks like it should be on the back of a cocktail napkin, it's probably too short. How can I make that allegation? Because, even if you're asking a quick question or giving an answer to one, email chicken scratching can be devoid of tone, feel and/or personality, thus often misconstrued. The exception to this rule is when the banter has been going back and forth—and you're in the midst of an ongoing repartee—or you're having a live dialogue using Instant Messaging or Text Messaging. That's different.

Naturally, very often the appropriate length can depend upon subject, message, request, directive, time factors—and the communication preferences you have established between you and your recipients. (You know how important I think that is.) But in general I believe there are some basic guidelines we should follow.

QUICK, FAST AND EASY

There is no argument that email has forced us to communicate differently than we used to, which means we need a new set of rules that accommodate such changes. What with the daily advances in new technologies such as cell phones, text messaging, computers, voice mails, and video conferencing, helping us to more efficiently hook up with others, most of the time we want our messages delivered quickly and easily. So how do we accomplish this and not under- or overdo in the process?

Let's start by looking at some basic email guidelines to determine what might be considered too long. Here's what I came up with:

YOUR EMAIL IS TOO LONG IF:

1. **It takes more than 20 seconds to read.** You'd better begin editing if your missive goes on and on. Most people I know who are email addicts have little patience to read long-winded emails. They can't wait to get on to the next one. Some say 10 seconds is enough, others 30 or 60. Do a little self test: Time your next incoming email and see how many seconds it takes for you to read it. I'm betting that when you reach the 30-second mark you will be antsy. What's your tolerance level? Govern your outgoing emails accordingly.

2. **You make the same point more than once.** We all need to state the issue/problem/need/solution clearly and succinctly. If you are saying the same thing in a variety of ways, it means the recipient has to spend time possibly reading and rereading your email to ferret out the heart of the message. Get to the point, make it once, and move on.

3. **A PDA user has to scroll down his screen more than four times to take in your message.** Remember who your audience is and stick with the serve-and-support rule. How does Jane or Joe like her/his email? Are they on a BlackBerry or sitting at their desk? Also, consider the pace at which your email colleagues operate on the job. How much time during the day do they spend with that PDA device? Is that how they get most of your email? What did they tell you when you gave them your "How do you like your email" survey? Most PDA users want their info short and sweet, but complete.

4. **You find out your recipient has gotten bored reading your emails.** If the person you're sending them to hints that your emails are a little tedious, or mentions

that to the guy sitting next to you, and that guy does you a favor by telling you what your coworker said, take the criticism constructively. Make your emails more succinct. Boring people by email is the same as boring people with too much verbal chatter. Whether it's verbal or written, ennui prevails when a person has to listen to someone drone on and on. Do your emails ramble and languish?

5. **Their mind begins to drift while in the midst of reading your email.** How can you tell? Maybe the Email Fairy will be kind enough to let you know. Or maybe you call up the person to whom you sent the email to follow up because you didn't hear back from her. You weren't sure your email went through. When you finally do speak to her, she says, "Oh yes, here it is, right here." Then she begins to read it. (And you can gauge how long it's taking if you pull it up on your screen and read it silently along with her.) If suddenly she starts talking about something else like a new job task, what she wants for lunch that day, or those damn Yankees, you know the length of your email has passed the "not very interesting" mark. It's no longer interesting because it's just too long! (Think of it like an overdone movie or play.)

6. **You've included too many attachments in one email.** When it takes a couple of minutes to download your sales report, your PowerPoint show and the photos of the new product line, most people will get annoyed because it takes too much time to read the initial email, store the documents, open them up and then read them. (Is it time to clock out yet?) Either send them separately (I'm not kidding) or provide links where they can click on them and read the materials instantly without going through all that rigmarole. Time seems to be a more precious commodity for

all corporate types than it used to be. Respect that. Continuing to send lengthy emails can provoke a "diss" connection between the two of you.

YOUR EMAIL IS TOO SHORT IF:

1. **People have to ask for clarification or further explanation.** Whether you initiated the email, are responding to one, or are in the middle of email banter, you must be specific while being concise. Fragmented information is often hard to discern and can very easily be misconstrued. These are the kinds of emails where people often get their feelings hurt. Slow down. Once again, look at your email communication from the perspective of the person who is receiving it.

2. **You do not demonstrate some tone or personality.** Because many of us are in a hurry we've gotten in the habit of sending cryptic email messages. In the process, we display (or convey) little, if any, human element. As a communicator it is your responsibility to connect. Down-and-dirty emails are usually void of "voice." The person on the other end must not only hear you but "feel" you and "read" you, too. Though you may disagree with this rule, I'm adamant about it. I have seen many a relationship fall apart because people were aloof, blunt and direct. One or two extra words might be all that is needed. Don't lose sight of "Do unto others…" Why not sign it, "Warmest regards," or open with "It's good to be in touch again," or add an inspiring quote of the day or a short humor bite?

3. **People see your email as some kind of attack.** I touched on this a moment ago. For instance, if someone emailed you to ask when you needed the

Dawson Report, and you emailed back "Right now," and that's all you said, it might be construed as a demand or harsh order. Adding the words "please" or "I appreciate it," may be all that is needed to stave off a bad vibe, one that can be perpetuated over time.

4. **It contains no real message.** I have seen many an email that could be interpreted as some arcane code from a spy. For example, "u know this time" is not a complete message, nor is "am there, maybe before." The problem with the super short message is that it is often ambiguous. By the time the receiver tries to figure out your purpose for emailing them (and they may have to email you several times to find out or even have to track you down on the phone or in person), you've both lost precious time. Don't forget "cut and paste" and the improv comedy player's precepts about "Creating into Certainty," and "Answering the Question." They fit nicely into the realm of etiquette for "It's too short if…"

5. **It's only one word.** The exception to this is when you are responding or receiving quick replies during an email banter. In that case one word may be appropriate, but to initiate an email with one word such as "help" leaves the receiver out in the cold. He doesn't know if you're being held at gunpoint, want assistance on a certain project, or need help finding an employee. Typically, one word is not enough unless, as I pointed out, you are simply *completing* a piece of communication with another emailer by saying "thnx" or "welcome."

6. **Your message comes across as impolite.** "Not now" or "Get someone else" are not nice things to say in an email. You probably wouldn't convey a message

quite like that to someone in person, so why do it in an email? This is not a rhetorical question, because most people who email these sorts of messages know that they don't have to deal with the person to whom they've sent the message. In other words, there will be no verbal response, usually. Most likely if you receive a follow-up email, you then get to make the choice of responding or ignoring their email. I'm sure it goes without saying that this email behavior falls well within the "Big Diss" category. What is really unfortunate is that I know people who say things like the phrases above with no intention of being impolite; they are just rushing to get a message to you. However, most people don't perceive short, curt messages in any other way than rude. Consciously or subconsciously, they feel they have been dissed. You can change all that by just adding a few words to a minimal message. An example? Consider two additional words, "Not now. So sorry." How about adding "Can you" to "Get someone else?" Always remember that etiquette equals good manners. We should strive to be polite to everyone. Also remember that you cannot read tone on paper, but you can express tone through words if you're a thoughtful enough writer (more on that in Chapter Five).

Hopefully, each of the above rules for "too long" and "too short" will give you a credo to lean on when composing those workplace emails.

FRAME OF REFERENCE

Taking a look at some "before" and "after" email correspondence always proves helpful in the *Bliss or "Diss"* workshop. With that in mind, I present just a couple of examples—ones that I hope will further clarify why I have chosen the 12 rules above and how they can be extremely helpful in guiding you.

Too long:

"I got the cartoon ideas yesterday and they look good but we need to revise a few of the ideas. I was thinking that we could use only two of the original ones and then choose between four or five for the others. Maybe I should run them by a few people at the office who like the guy sitting behind the desk instead of the guy in front of it because they helped me pick the first ones. I always think cartoons work better if everyone laughs, but sometimes only a few people laugh and others feel left out. I remember feeling left out in fifth grade when someone drew this stick figure and it didn't have clothes on it and everyone thought it was funny but I didn't get it because I thought stick figures didn't have clothes anyway, ever, so I didn't know why everyone was laughing. My mom was always careful not to buy me any Christmas funny things that had stick figures on them because she knew it would remind me and then I would feel bad. I guess if you want to give me some more ideas before we start to make choices that could be a smarter way to go. I think I like two of them but we should look at four to five others before we make a final decision. The guys at the office always have great ideas and I think I should run things by them before we talk again. I would call but I don't want to take up time when I don't know. Asking the guys will help because they always see things I don't see and they say two heads are better than one, or in my case, three or four heads are better than one. How about if I call you in a couple of days and when I have time to run these by the guys and see what they have to say. I bet you could come up with other good ideas if they don't like these because I know how creative you are. I have attached five of my own and I also attached some ideas a few guys at the office emailed over. Hope they help you. They're not very good drawings but I hope you get the idea. Since I paid one price to you with no limit I might ask you to do that. I have to ask the guys what they think first. Hope you have a nice day. Beth"

Poor Beth! But then again, Poor Email Recipient. Had I been her intended, I would not have answered until I had hit the nearest saloon and thrown back a shot or two of Jack Daniels! (And I don't even drink.) Yes, poor, pitiful Beth. Unknowingly, she violates just about every *Bliss or "Diss"* rule in the "too-long" category.

First, the buzzer would have sounded in terms of length. Her email took more than a minute to read. I clocked it. And, the content was redundant. She made the same point about running the cartoons in question by her colleagues five times. If her recipient was on a PDA and that device had a built in Smith and Wesson, by the time he got to the fifth-grade incident, he probably would have put the PDA to his head. Had Beth gone back over the email before firing it off (which 90 percent of people DO NOT do) she may have realized that she had a serious editing job before her. You don't have to ask her recipient if he was getting bored. I'm sure he watched a good portion of the first quarter of the basketball game on ESPN to break things up before he got to the end of her message. As for the number of attachments included, the receiver could have made dinner and eaten it in the same amount of time it took him to download and look over them.

Here is the same email, redone:

"Got your cartoon ideas yesterday and thanks. I like two of the original ones, but would like to run the others by the guys at the office before I make a final selection for the remaining four or five. They always have great input. Would like the cartoons to be ones that will make everyone laugh, not just a few people. (Remind me to tell you a story about me and stick figures and fifth grade sometime.) Since I paid one price with no limitations I might ask you to whip up a few new ideas based on what the guys have to say. I have some samples to get to you. Do you want them as attachments, copy and paste, pdf's or faxes? Have a nice day, Beth."

This is certainly a vast improvement. You can pare this down even more—make it shorter and sweeter. (I'm big on brevity but not at the expense of losing intent or tone. More on that in our next chapter.)

SHORT, SWEET AND SOMETIMES POINTLESS

Now let's take a look at a before/after version of an email that falls into the "too short" slot. Here it is:

"Get me that file. Not with D.R. letter. John's on my back. Hurry this time. Jim."

Well, that was certainly short and sweet, but its contents butt up against much of the decorum I laid out in the "too short if…" listings. First off, it represents another classic example of "dissing." Secondly, the person to whom the "order" was given probably had to ask for clarification on what "that" file meant and also ask for an explanation of what "D.R." stood for. This was certainly not a clear message. The receiver may have been willing to be more helpful if she had understood why Frank needed the file and why so quickly. With that information, she may have been able to support him in ways that he may not have thought of. Closing with "hurry *this* time" infers that the recipient dropped the ball a previous time. That's hurtful. Now, maybe Frank did not mean to degrade anyone, but when you can't hear the person speak (no tone/personality) the words take on their own meaning. So, words need to be chosen carefully. Maybe in his own head he thought he was pleading in a kind way. Maybe he was attempting to be funny. We honestly don't know because neither kindness nor humor came through. For the sake of argument, let me present two revamped versions, the first is delivered more clearly and kindly; the second shows how humor could have been conveyed, if that's what Frank had intended.

"Candy,
Will you kindly get me the Johnson file — the first one (not the file
with the direct report letter in it). John's calling in ten minutes
to quiz me on it! Please, oh please, do one of your fantastic
turnarounds for me. Thanks in advance! Jim."

As you can see, it is still short, but conveys a clearer
message and, if she's insightful, offers Candy the opportunity
to gather up anything else she thinks Frank might need. She
also is made to feel appreciated and respected.

Here's the short version with a humorous approach:

"Candy,
John's calling in ten minutes (Heaven help us!). I desperately need
(picture me, I'm on my knees) the Johnson file — the one without
the direct report letter. Need it fire-engine-fast! I'm begging...I'm
already grateful to you! Yikes... please...hurry...(If it's more than
five minutes from now, look for me outside the window. I'll be
the one standing on the ledge!) Jim"

I've written many books on the subject of using humor
in speeches, communications and in the workplace, and I
continue to believe that there is nothing more conducive to
bonding, strengthening relationships and relieving stress
than appropriately applied humor. It would be hard for
Candy to deny Frank quick assistance with this approach.
In this version, Frank allows himself to be vulnerable and
he shares his sheer panic, but in such a fun way. Humor
is enchanting, charming and hard to resist. Though this
email is much longer than the initial version, it does offer
a specific message and better clarifies Frank's needs. It also
shows appreciation and respect. I will always opt for a little
more message in order to solidify a human connection. How
about you?

FINAL THOUGHTS

As homework, I am asking that you review at least five incoming and five outgoing—those you've written—emails. Following the rules I've laid out in this chapter, chop down the long ones, and add to, soften and humanize the short ones. These exercises will help bring home my messages in a very concrete way. Sure, you can cop out on this assignment by saying you will always heed these rules from this time forward. But as a writer—and teacher of different types of writing styles—I know there is nothing more effective in getting the lessons across than having students take already written material and rework it.

In this chapter I have put forth some edicts on the "long and short" of emails. In the next chapter I will present some ideas on how to make you a better communicator through your written word. While you may already be a capable writer, I will show you how to delve more deeply into writing style, content choices, writing ethics and how to get "voice" into your emails. I will share with you a good deal of what I have learned as a publicist, copywriter, comedy writer and author, for I believe these insights will help you write email communications that establish, build and maintain those business relationships that are so vital to you.

Chapter Five

GOOD OR BAD?
Writing well; writing poorly.

Like it or not, to be a good emailer, you need to be a good writer.

I mentioned earlier in the book that the email dilemma presents a whole new set of problems to those of us who do most of our business communicating in writing. Granted, we want to stay conversational, but we also need to come across as professional. Words are powerful and how you put them together in an email can make the difference between *no* sale and *the* sale, as well as *no* relationship and a *good* relationship.

Good writing; hmmm, sounds feasible, but how do you make it happen? That is what this chapter is all about. It will lay out some tricks, shortcuts (I know how you love them!), and some secrets used by publicists, advertising copy writers, journalists, feature writers, sketch and stand-up comedy writers, playwrights and screenwriters to help guide you in composing better emails.

HATS OFF, PERIOD

If you're an articulate and well-mannered grammarian, I salute you. You may not need this chapter, although I would like you to humor the rest of us and do the assignments anyway. For you English majors, they'll be fun! For those of you who are top-notch writers, hats off to you, too. In fact, feel free to skip this section of the book if you like. Go out and spread the gospel of *Bliss or "Diss"* or get a latte or something. Everyone else, read on.

A SECOND LANGUAGE

For those of you who are still with me, let's start in the English department—with mechanics, that is. Next I'll tackle content and style.

I hate to report this, but the worst email writers I have come across—in terms of a near disregard for language arts—include the younger generation. They're great with computers and gadgets, but they have openly and unashamedly confessed to little interest in English 101. I don't mean to bash the younger set. Many CEOs and top-level managers fall into the same slot. I cannot begin to tell you how many Top Dogs and Big Cheeses have poor English skills. I work with them every day. I'm not exactly sure why some people adhere to the philosophy: "Who cares how I compose it? I just write and click." But I know that's the norm in many instances because I've been assessing my students' email writing skills ever since I offered my first *Bliss or "Diss"* class. I've noticed that paying attention to proper grammar, using correct punctuation and making sophisticated vocabulary choices are sorely lacking in emails. However, when many of these same individuals are asked to write a formal letter, they often seem to craft it with a little more respect and consideration. Why? Because, to them, that's different. Because somebody, an English teacher, for example, gave us rules for how to write formal correspondence. Because the part of the inherent magic of this new communication medium—email—is that it is slick and quick, and most business professionals who use it are the types who run their workdays on speed dial. They need to get from one business task to the next, fast—*really* fast. So, forget attention to "language arts!" And, besides, they see their colleagues doing the same thing. So why should they do anything different?

SOME AGREEMENT

Yes to all that, but I think the real problem is something else. If we go back to square one, we can see that it's all part of the *absence of guidelines* for email etiquette. There *is* no mandate for well-written verbiage in email. There is no email police and so, like rioters, email perpetrators are free to roam the streets of cyberspace tossing a preposition, a conjunction and/or an interjection through an email message if they feel like it. They can slam down a period if and when the mood strikes them, ram their information at will through fragments, phrases or clauses, pillage the symbol drawer with :)s, LOLs, BTWs and @s, kick out words with misspellings, and recklessly slaughter the structure of sentences. Sometimes there are caps, other times no caps. Occasionally, there is an ellipsis, other times a sentence is left dangling. And, please, someone tell me, doesn't a question mark still go with a question?

Apart from basic grammatical errors, how about composition?

ASKING IS VERY TELLING

One of the first questions I ask when we get to the workshop segment that deals with the do's and don'ts of composing emails, is how many people in the class are professional writers. About two percent say yes. The rest are business professionals who do not work in marketing, advertising or public relations, or for print, broadcast or Internet media.

Two percent professional writers, overall, is troubling to me as a communications specialist and professional writer because I am keenly aware of how strongly our written messages impact others, for good or ill; and, as I have already mentioned, how much we rely on email to do business. I'm not suggesting we all have to be professional writers to log on, but as a group we should have reasonable English skills, some decorum and outright good manners when at the helm of the keyboard and we should also pay attention to the way we compose our emails, making sure they are well-crafted.

ARE YOU IMPRESSED?

As email-oholics we make lasting impressions on others as a result of our writing skills. You may argue that BlackBerry and text messaging have changed all that, but I think the jury is still out on that one. Perhaps there is a lot more leeway in writing finesse when sending a cryptic message because such emails are meant to convey information in bites, but I'm more concerned about the typical email message that is sent from computer to computer, even within the same office.

Go back over your emails of this week. How many of them contain a word that is misspelled or misused? How many have run-on sentences (like the email from Beth in our last chapter), poor grammar, or sloppy punctuation? How many demonstrate a limited vocabulary?

I'm not suggesting that you have to write like a feature writer for *The New Yorker* or become as tight and clean an author as John Grisham, but you do need to think about how you are received and perceived if email is how you put yourself out there in the professional business world. And most of us do, through email.

We've all heard admonishments from employment agencies, headhunters, college professors and, yes, our mothers and fathers about how important first impressions are. This admonishment has particular relevance to emailers because for many of us who rely on email, writing a message and sending it is the way we make our first impressions. And when things don't go so well, our last impression!

Not only that, but you make an impression with *every* email you send.

You project an identity with every email you send.

You connect or disconnect with every email you send.

Perhaps I'm especially sensitive when it comes to creating a strong personal image through email because even though I have always been enormously creative, I did not start out with good mechanics. Actually, I flunked dumbbell English (I thought I was going to be a movie star), and it wasn't until I fell in love with comparative literature and started writing seriously that I scrambled to learn the fundamentals. Today, I am tremendously aware that how I present myself in email is how people will perceive me. I want them to think I'm unusually creative, yes, but I also want them to think I am polished, professional and articulate. They will only get that impression if my emails reflect those qualities. I share this background with you because it took me a long time to get my language arts down and to learn to become a good writer. If you're behind in your general skills, don't worry; you can always acquire or brush up on them.

WRITER'S WRITERS

Let's move on to some discussion about content. I teach many writing classes and always prepare my students who think writing is going to be a snap by sharing this caveat: writing is *rewriting*. I don't know of any worthwhile or successful writers—from journalists to playwrights—who haven't told me that they have gone through several drafts to get to their final product.

Obviously, I know most of us are not going to do several drafts of a piece of email correspondence, but if we learn to be better writers—take lessons and tips from those who write every day for a living—our emails will display better form, structure and composition. Gaining in skill means that when we sit down to write an email, we will have gotten into some very good habits—patterns that will consistently fall into place when we put fingertips to keyboard. Ah, yes, we will develop routines that will ultimately pay off in terms of making a positive and powerful impression. (Remember, we're all selling something.)

Editing and rewriting can be challenging at first, but it gets easier even though it requires focus and dedication. Husband #2, the late Bud Furillo, who was one of southern California's most revered sportswriters, an excellent columnist and a broadcaster, used to tell me that you had to "suffer" to be a good writer. At the time, I laughed in his face! I even mocked him. I scoffed at the idea. But he was right. And even today as I go over my copy, I rework it until it shines, whether it is a press release, a feature story, ad copy, brochure or memoir. (The latter made me realize why Hemingway shot himself!)

I'm not suggesting that you should pore over every word of every email, but I am asking that you view your "copy" differently from this point forward by adhering to some of the same secrets, tips and "rules" used by many writers as they work with their content.

I will let you in on how these professionals approach their writing assignments because I think such insights might get you thinking about how you can better craft your email messages.

BACK TO BASICS

Before I move forward into more detail about writers and their approaches to content, here are just a few easy-to-remember guidelines if you want your messages to be more English-proper:

1. <u>**Make sure your grammar and spelling are correct**</u>. Whether your messages contain complete sentences or phrases, this is very important. We all have

spell and grammar check so there shouldn't be any excuses. Nothing says, "I'm still in third grade" faster and better than copy that is full of these types of errors.

2. **<u>Check your punctuation</u>.** Leaving off periods, apostrophes, colons, question marks, commas and other such marks are like driving down the street with no road signs. The reader needs them for quick and easy assimilation and *you* need them to make a good impression, one that says, "I'm full pro." (I don't care if you are in a hurry!)

3. **<u>Check your vocabulary</u>.** Do you overuse the same adjectives and adverbs? Do you say "very" and "really" throughout your messages? These are called intensifiers and they become meaningless when constantly repeated. Do your word choices come across as "well said?" You want to choose words that make you sound intelligent, yet are easy for the average emailer to understand. Vocabulary is an area that you don't want to overdo or underdo. When selecting the "right" words for your messages, consider your audience (serve and support). Be versatile, depending upon the person to whom you are writing. To expand your ability to express yourself, learn three new words a day. You'll be surprised at how much more expressive your emails can become. People tend to respect those who have a broader vocabulary. But, don't go to extremes. You don't want to sound like an erudite (that mean's "scholarly") snob. You also don't want to overuse the thesaurus because people will know when you're reaching. For example, if today you wrote, "I will call you to talk about our HR problem with Brad. I agree, he has been supercilious and obdurate." Whoa! Better to simply say, "...I agree, he has been arrogant

and inflexible." Remember, your email is "talking for you." Don't use words you would not use in general conversation. The only people I know who use highbrow words are English professors, C-Span interviewers and butlers in English movies that were made in the 40s. Always consider variety because it is more important in written communication than it is when speaking in person. Take a look at some of the emails you sent today. Were your descriptions weak and colorless because the words you chose were flat or vague? Did you keep using the same words over and over again? Did you use words that were far too intellectual and completely out of place?

4. **Take a second pass at your email message before you push "send."** Does it have any typos? Any awkward sentences? Does your message reflect polished mechanics? Even though spell check did not give you a red underline when you typed the word "pear," maybe you meant to spell it "pair," or "pare"? Don't be lazy, reread your emails. There's nothing more embarrassing than having the client call you on the misspelled or wrong word choice. Don't be an email fool!

5. **Break your email into separate paragraphs.** If the email message you're sending has more than a few sentences in it, distinguish one idea from another by putting spaces between each idea. That way, they are easier and faster to take in. Paragraphs also help you divide one thought from another, which makes your copy more precise and your message evident.

As silly as this may sound, if you're not adept in the English department, grab a few reference books and use them to learn some basics—the ones you probably slept through in grammar school. I have several of them. My favorite (don't laugh) is a book written for sixth to eighth graders, *Painless Grammar* by Rebecca Elliott, Ph.D. When I purchased it, I had no idea that was the audience for whom Prof Elliott had written it. I didn't realize that until six months later. Oh, well, it gets the job done for me when I'm in question. What will you use?

SO MANY WRITERS, SO LITTLE TIME

Good writers not only have good skills, they have great style. It would be ideal if each of us not only had solid language arts, but if we could develop a trademark in the way we put our words across...wow!

Every professional writer I know, whether they are hardcore journalists (just the facts, nothing but the facts kind of writers) or stand-up comedy writers (their words have punch), works at making their writing brand identifiable. Hunter S. Thompson, Bob Woodward and Art Buchwald are three writers whose work I have long admired. Advertising geniuses such as Jerry Della Femina and William Bernbach are two others whose writing really stands out in my mind. In the comedy genre, Dave Chappelle and Ellen DeGeneres are only two of the writers whose work has a unique and unmistakable quality. Edward Albee and David Mamet are two of the best playwright/screenwriters to put words to scripts. Who do you like?

I often tell my aspiring writing students to spend as much time reading those they admire as they do honing their own style. It not only helps novices and even good writers become *better* writers, it also provides an opportunity to analyze why they enjoy reading their work. For instance, I always enjoy Dominick Dunne, who writes columns for *Vanity Fair* on crimes of the rich and famous. They are simple and easy to assimilate, but always compelling in the way they are presented. In the magazine's November, 2006 issue in his column on the JonBenét Ramsey case, he writes, "From the moment I saw John Mark Karr on television, looking like a dainty Lee Harvey Oswald in a pale-blue

Nautica shirt and high-waisted trousers, I felt strongly that he hadn't done it, but I wanted to believe he had."

MAKE YOUR LIST

If you're interested in becoming a better writer—and you should be if you're going to use email regularly for business purposes—I ask that you make a list of those writers you most enjoy and respect. Take another pass at their work. Study how they put their words together.

In addition, go through your "old" emails from others and see which ones you consider interesting and well-written and which ones you view as embarrassing. Be honest, whether you are making an assessment of people you truly respect or those for whom you don't have a great regard. Be as objective as you can about how they craft their emails to you.

I don't want to get too heavy-handed with you in the "improve-your-writing" department, but as you can see I have devoted an entire chapter to this subject because as a communications specialist, I think it's critical that we all master the fundamentals in both mechanics and form if we spend the majority of our business day sending emails. So please do this homework. You might even try to come up with some other writing evaluation exercises you create on your own.

WRITING CLASS

To round out this chapter, I will share with you different types of writers and writing styles. Many of their approaches can be utilized in creating effective emails. I've broken my examples into writing categories. By learning a handful of writers' tricks and secrets and seeing how they approach their work, I think you'll pick up a few new pointers on how to make your own writing stronger.

Look closely at their principles—the ones they follow to make their copy so focused and so easy to grasp. Also, ponder what they do to give their messages impact and punch.

"AD" TO THIS

1. <u>Advertising</u>: If they are any good, these writers can pack quite a punch or deliver a profound message in just a few words. They are always thinking taglines (McDonald's: "You deserve a break today." Budweiser: "True." United Dairy Council: "Got Milk?" Nissan: "Driven." These writers opt for short and definitive messages, the shorter the better, yet they never sacrifice their message for brevity. Each message must pack a wallop.

   How can their writing benefit you? Think about the message in your subject line. Is it exact, direct and descriptive? What about the body of your email? If you are the type of email addict who's in a huge hurry, those short direct sentences or phrases you're spewing out should be complete ideas—ones that are explicit.

   Another trick up the ad copywriter's sleeve is that he or she is always trying to get the reader to act. "Call to action" is how we commonly refer to this technique, when a writer wants the reader to be instantly motivated or inspired to buy. Yes, they do it through visuals such as showing the close up of the ice cold Coca Cola can with beads of condensation dripping down it, but they also do it with words, sometimes only one, such as Budweiser: "True." That's why you react to ads, whether they are in print, broadcast media, pop-ups on the Internet or plastered on billboards. For examples, "Coke: The Real Thing", Nike: "Just Do It", Capitol One: "What's In Your Wallet?"

   As an email-oholic who probably rushes from one email to another, how can you effectively get your message across in a few hard-hitting and exact words? Study the work of the advertising copywriter. Their approach to advertising has a lot to do with your approach to getting your point across quickly and pointedly. For the BlackBerry and text message user, understanding their approach will be a godsend to you! The library or any bookstore has wonderful books on writing ad copy.

THE BIG SPIN

2. <u>**Public Relations**</u>: This type of writer is the opposite of the ad copywriter. He is more interested in offering information in a way that is embellished and highly descriptive. A press release might include news, yes, but it is often delivered in a more elaborate manner. For instance, the description in a press release about the lobby of a new office suite might include phrases such as "…a sweeping panoramic view of the city" or "Each office suite features a décor of authentic earth tones with dramatically rich teak hardwood floors, Victorian-era silk window coverings…" and so forth. Client biographies are not only data-specific, but hit on the human interest aspect of a personality, using phrases such as "He is not only a gifted speaker and dynamic leader, but he also is known for his ingenious strategies in handling celebrity crises, qualities that have won him numerous awards." Note the use of adjectives. P.R. writers are big on adjectives.

   To better define the differences between the two types of writers—advertising and P.R.—I often point out to my students that the ad copywriter makes you "act" and the P.R. copywriter makes you "feel." If you like to write lengthier emails, take notice of the P.R. writer's style (though such writers are now opting for shorter press releases and more condensed press kits because many a client now has their kit info on a website). Their style is often designed not only to be "newsy," but is occasionally geared to stimulate mood. Often the P.R. writer brings personality to *things,* not just people.

Study the publicists' work. They are the great "connectors" in the world of communications, the people who take information from one source and connect it to another that distributes it widely to the public. They know how to cleverly "spin" their messages, skillfully getting us to view a situation or person a certain way. Go online and Google some major companies or events and read through their press releases. You might pick up a tip or two. Do any of your emails need to include detail? Do you need to persuade and motivate others? (Who doesn't!)

Repeat the homework assignment above, but this time review your own recent emails. Are the longer ones descriptive and interesting? Do they segue well from one idea to another? Do they contain a subject line that grabs your attention, like the snappy headline used by publicists? (One example comes to mind. I recently created a fundraiser for a client. Several celebrities donated jerseys and shirts for the event. The headline read: "Stars Give Shirts Off Backs For Peace.") Do you express yourself adequately through those emails? If there is room for improvement, redo a few of them. You might be very pleased with your edits.

HARD OR SOFT NEWS

3. **Journalists:** These types of writers may be reporters of "just the facts," or they may be those who write what we call "features." Factual reporting is the style used in the *Wall Street Journal* while feature articles can be seen in the news stories often found in magazines such as *Time.* In either case, both styles hone in on giving the reader important news,

whether they do so in a simple "who, what, why, where, when," format or expound on a story, digging deeper into a news angle in more detail.

Examine both formats for style. Whether it's a newspaper, magazine or Internet article, observe how succinctly the hard news reporter puts his or her information across, while the soft news or feature writer takes the liberty of further explanation. Feature writers are especially good at providing in-depth coverage by citing examples, making comparisons, and providing history and background on a person, place or thing.

You guessed it. Once again, review your email correspondence and ask yourself these questions: When should you report just the facts? When is it appropriate to delve into your subject and paint a broader picture? Also, take note of whether or not your content flows. Does it unfold sequentially, connecting one salient point to another, or do you meander round and round, trying to report your news? Study the journalists, for they are the masters of compiling information, organizing it methodically and keeping us interested as we read it. In time, you can write emails with the same skill.

FUNNY THING HAPPENED

4. <u>Sketch Comedy Writers</u>: These folks write satire, my favorite form of creative writing, on any and everything. In my book that teaches sketch writing, *Build to Laugh: How to Construct Sketch Comedy with the Fast and Funny Formula,* I tell my students that they must answer one question before they embark on any piece: "What's the point?" or stated somewhat differently, "Where's the joke?" We can learn a good deal from this group of artisans because their writing emanates from those criteria. How many times do we veer off course or never get to the point

in our emails? If, like the sketch writer, we identify that point from the get-go and construct an email message that builds on it, fleshing it out, we stand a better chance of providing clear messages to the recipient. Sketch writers also work with what we call "beat points," pivotal, turning or transition points that take the scene from one juncture to the next. If your emails are rampant with non sequiturs or if one piece of information doesn't flow sensibly to the next, try studying the construction of sketches. They're tight. Just like an email, a sketch has to be short, yet it has to tell a complete story—one that backs up the overall point of the satirical jab.

STAND UP AND PACK SOME PUNCH

5. **Standup Comedy Writing:** These folks are usually working toward one goal: the punchline. They have to set up the joke, then service it incrementally, building it until they reach the end where that final word or line has to deliver on the initial promise: a humorous kick. Taking stock of their writing style is interesting because the listener is compelled to take in every line in order to understand and reach the finish line. Pull out those emails of yours again. Do any of them start with a tidbit of intriguing information? Do you build on that fodder, enticing your audience to read your entire email (so long as it's not too long)? I think the standup comedy writer has a tough assignment, for every joke requires a setup and a high impact ending. How do you end your emails? Do they trail off? Do you provide the interesting message in your opening line, then digress it to death, thus boring the reader? Take just one of your emails and write it from the standup comedy writer's rulebook. Open with a tease and lure the recipient. Deliver on your promise of a big

finish. Your email recipients may not know why they are so eager to click and read your incoming missives, but you will.

PLAY RIGHT, LIKE THEM

6. **Playwrights:** Whether they are writing for screen or the stage, the work of the playwright features another interesting format. They have to tell an entire story in a relatively short period of time. A stage play is usually no more than three acts and usually one and a half hours in length. A screenplay is much the same in theory and typically the script is no more than 120 pages, each page equaling a minute — two hours of film time. While playwrights are intrinsically no different from the writers I have described above, they do vary in one important respect. They pay particular attention to the characters and their development throughout the storytelling process. The part of their work from which you can gain some wisdom is the fact that each character has to say a good deal, but most often in relatively few words. This group of writers is very adept at adhering to the "Economy of Dialogue" rule. Every word has to count. You may not have noticed this because you've been so wrapped up in the story and the people in it. What I find most fascinating about the playwright is that he always leaves you wanting more.

What we can learn from this group of wordsmiths is conciseness, clarity, a focus on the significance of the message and the importance of getting to know people. I have said throughout this book that our email messages are continually misconstrued. In a successful play, whether for screen or stage, that is never the case. Just for fun, get a copy of a script and read only one scene. Note how much is revealed in just a few pages, how succinct and crisp the dialogue is. Now rewrite an email or two of your own and approach them from the playwright's vantage point. Make your message incisive and project your personality. Let the recipient receive insights into you, the character. Tell a good story.

BEG, BORROW AND STEAL

All in all, writers borrow aspects of style from one another. Former feature writer and playwright/screenwriter, Alan Ball, is a good example. Writer of the highly-acclaimed film, *American Beauty*, Ball was once a writer for *Adweek* and *PR Insider* magazine. He built on what he had learned as a feature writer and adapted one format and applied it to screenwriting, creating fast-moving and tightly-worded scenes that accomplished a great deal in a short amount of time. He made every word count. Less is more.

You can do the same.

If you study the work of the playwright and each of the other writing styles I presented, and use some of the same techniques and approaches they use with their daily assignments, you will find that your email communication has more clarity, meaning, style and sophistication—and when you want it, more heart and punch. Blend these ingredients all together or choose just one category that resonates with you to develop your very own email writing style. I am absolutely convinced that you can become a better emailer by studying the work of professional writers, so don't slough off on this assignment. Remember, if you are an email addict, you're going to conduct much of your business using that medium, which means doing much of your selling of ideas, products, services etc. in writing. Shouldn't your content be representative of a fully professional businessperson, one that impresses others?

THE CLOSER

In summary, here are a few simple etiquette guidelines

for email content. Your content:

1. must be clear
2. must have a sequence to it, one idea logically following another
3. must have style, your own individual touch
4. must contain as few words as possible without sacrificing the message
5. must make a point
6. must include personality
7. must be intriguing, interesting or compelling
8. must make a favorable impression
9. must be easy to assimilate
10. must leave them wanting more

Take time to follow these principles. Though I know your time is valuable, read over your emails before sending them. Make edits if necessary. Remember what I said earlier, good writing is rewriting! It will get easier with practice, believe me.

Let's move on to the following chapter where I will provide some etiquette as to what is naughty and what is nice in terms of email content and substance.

Chapter Six

RIGHT OR WRONG?
Being naughty; making nice?

Nothing is worse than the Great American Corporate "Diss," —not having your email answered—except for getting one that makes you mad or hurts your feelings. I've had those days when I could kick myself for ever having cursed those times I'd been email "dissed." Though I don't like that at all, at least it may be better to have someone ignore me entirely than to have them answer me with a curt, cold or, yes, even painfully cruel email.

Cold? Cruel? Yep, these emails fly back and forth from the minute Corporate America brews that first cup of coffee till the final elevator empties out its last load of blurry-eyed workers.

TAKING SIDES

I want to be an optimist. I want to believe in my fellow man/woman as a compassionate species, but there ought to be rules about what you can and cannot say in an email, or at least some etiquette about fundamental demeanor in them. Some use email as an opportunity to say hurtful

95

things. Things they would not otherwise say to someone's face or over the phone. That's wrong (naughty). Email does not give any of us a license to blast our business colleagues and coworkers, to hurt or criticize them, then click the mouse and run.

I do want to err on side of humanity, though. I want to believe that *most* businesspersons would never overtly use email as a weapon in workplace psychological warfare. (Okay, there are some who do, and you and I know them.) But wars *do* start because of the manner in which messages are delivered in emails. While some missives are covertly and/or intentionally nasty, I truly believe the majority of them are not. However, the fact remains, many people get into tiffs with one another, harbor resentments or even end long-term relationships because of naughty emails.

That's absolutely unnecessary.

In Chapter One and also in the "Don't Ever…" and "Always Do…" sections in Chapter Three, I covered a few rules mandating that you contact an individual in person or by phone if you have a criticism or complaint, or if you are having a misunderstanding, conflict or confrontation with them, rather than doing so by email. Let's say you're pretty good at doing that, or have become better at it since reading *Bliss or "Diss."* Good for you. I have to say, though, that as an email society we still have a ways to go. As business professionals we have to learn to recognize *when* we are sending a nice or naughty email.

SAY WHAT?

What I find most distressing as I sift through emails during class—those written by my students—is that many of those who compose them have no idea that the way they've posited their messages could, and possibly have been, taken the wrong way. I'm puzzled by this because students complain to me and the rest of the class about the emails *they* get—some of which are even nicer than the naughty ones they have sent! *Bingo!* That's the root of the problem. As a group, most of us don't outwardly intend to zing someone. It's just that we have no clue that some of the messages we're sending into cyperspace are simply being misunderstood on the other end. If we could get a collective grip on that unfortunate reality, we might start paying more attention to how our emails are perceived and then do something about it. Until then, I'm afraid that the "diss" in disconnection is going to become even more pronounced.

In one portion of my workshop, the students and I read the emails they have sent, first silently, then out loud to the rest of the class. (There's a whole lot of incredulous laughter!) That's when they begin to understand how and why people could misinterpret their intent. I wish I had a dollar for every time a student said, "But that isn't what I meant."

Next, we do the same exercise with the emails they have received from others. There's a lot of grumbling, then more laughter, then forgiveness. It's a real mind-blower!

THREE LITTLE WORDS, OR FOUR OR FIVE...

The root cause of email misinterpretation is simple: Sometimes it's just the words we choose. It can be something as ridiculous as one word that changes the intent of an email from pleasant to harsh. For example, if someone writes, "Don't call me before ten," that sounds a little austere, almost demanding. If instead they write, "Please don't call me before ten," or "Call after ten, please," that can make all the difference, can't it? The words *sound* different.

In class, we take one phrase and come up with as many variations in tone as we can think of. We move words around like we are playing Scrabble. In the process, everyone in class learns how powerful words really are and how the arrangement of them can make for either naughty or nice communication.

Then we conquer something else: subtext.

While words are critically important, subtext has the

dominant power. Subtext is what is not said in words, but expressed in tone.

Subtext always lies beneath the surface of every word we speak and it certainly comes across in every word we write.

Of course, conveying intent is easier with the spoken word. If you're a good listener, and can hear beneath the surface, you can really tell where someone is coming from, even if their remarks are antithetical to their mood. When they say, for instance, "I'm having a great day," with a tone of ennui or one of sarcasm, you quickly get the *real* message. Yet when they write that remark, the meaning of the words is up to your interpretation.

Can you understand how *your* emails might be misinterpreted? Can you also understand how important it is to be very specific with your tone so that your message will come across as intended? Great! That's a good start.

UP FOR GRABS

Context has a lot to do with how the information in your emails will be understood. In most cases, the receiver will attach his or her own meaning to the subtext, depending upon previous email correspondence, as well as the other language you use in your email before or after such phrases as "I'm having a great day." Another important factor in interpreting subtext is the nature of your ongoing relationship. If two people know each other fairly well, their emails will be relatively easy to interpret. Also, if you have spoken with a person regularly, or talked to them even once, you will more easily be able to sense the tone that lies beneath their email words. How someone sounds—their attitude, tempo and phrasing—all that carries over when you suddenly read their words in an email. You can almost *hear* that person speak as you read, can't you? Then again, there are still times when a person you know sends you an email that offends, hurts or angers you. That's particularly hard to deal with when the message comes from a person you work with every day. That worries me because, as I pointed out earlier, business relationships can fall apart over one poorly crafted email.

The greatest danger of misunderstanding lies in *new* relationships that have been established and maintained exclusively via email. You're already communicating at a disadvantage if you've only been in touch by email because one ill-toned message (even if you didn't mean it) can end your business relations with someone. Yes, trying to establish a new relationship via email is tricky because you have no history or former communication, so very often, interpretation is up for grabs.

ACTING OUT

When I first begin to train speakers or improv actors, I tackle the area of self-expression to ensure that their performances have "contrast" and "variety"—in other words, some depth—and that they are getting exactly the response they wish to evoke from the audience. I tell my students that creating a range of moods as they go along in a speech is not only very entertaining, but also clarifies the intent of their message. As I mentioned in Chapter One, to reinforce this, we give each student ten different sentences and a corresponding list of 180 different moods. As they read each one of the sentences in 180 attitudes, it is incredible to see how subtext can completely change the message.

Every word we utter—whether it is said out loud or written—has subtext for good or ill. Try saying, "I want that report by noon" ten different ways. Choose moods that are both naughty and nice. Say it through clenched teeth. Say it with a smile. Say it with excitement. Say it with nonchalance. Enlightening, isn't it? Well, just know that such a sentence in an email can be taken many different ways, depending on what sentences precede or follow it, and the tone contained in *those* words.

It's all about tone, "voice," whether spoken or written.
The tone we use always reflects an attitude.
Attitude can be a good or a bad thing.
There is attitude in every email we write and every email we receive.

ASK A WAY

The question I want you to ask yourself is this: what attitude do I convey? With me it changes from email to email, depending upon the situation (probably for you, too), yet I always try to be very explicit in my tone. I choose words and assemble them in a way that makes my message exactly reflect the attitude I wish to express. My goal is to keep that attitude positive, regardless of the nature of the missive. My focus is always on attitude first, and the words that will communicate it second. You can't go wrong if your intention (attitude) is crystal clear in your mind.

You may think that what I'm saying seems obvious. However, I have discovered from teaching email workshops that even though you may *think* the other person will get whatever "feel" you meant to attach to your message (cordiality, urgency, sympathy, understanding, humor), there are many instances throughout the day when, I promise you, your intent will be completely misconstrued — your message will not be received in the way you intend it to be. Creating the right tone in an email is something we must all learn to do through practice and awareness.

SNOTTY OR SWEET

I challenge you to look at the emails you've sent today and decide if your subtext is naughty or nice. What did you convey in terms of mood? Were you genuinely nice? Were you a little naughty, displaying a hint of hostility, sarcasm or irritation? Did you take the time (it doesn't take that long) to think carefully about how to pose your requests or inquiries, or did you just shoot them off spontaneously without giving them a second read to make sure they came across in a "connectable" way? (Most of us *are* in a hurry since the email addict is typically functioning on speed dial.)

In addition, for one day, take note of the attitude that is present in *all* written communication that comes your way, not just email. I don't care whether you will be reading a billboard message, the hype on the back of a cereal box, a newspaper article or a poem. You'll begin to understand what I'm talking about and the power of the messages that can be projected, depending on how the words are strung together and, more importantly, the kind of tone that bolsters them.

GOLDEN RULES

Though I have covered a number of etiquette rules for writing effective emails, here are a few more guidelines that focus strictly on the words you select and the tone that accompanies them.

Add these to your *Bliss or "Diss"* repertoire:

1. **<u>Choose your words wisely</u>.** Instead of "Not now," how about "Maybe a little later"? Rather than "You shouldn't have said that," how about "It may have been better not to say it quite that way"? How we select and arrange our words impacts our relationships greatly.

2. **<u>Reread your email objectively</u>.** Make necessary changes—a word here, a word there—to make your message effective and rid it of any hint of disrespect or discourtesy. Sure you may have a gripe with someone and you want to express it but, as I instructed in Chapter Three, don't email your complaint, instead get off your lazy butt and call or

show up in person to deliver it. Put *your* email shoe on the other foot. If you were the other guy, would you like receiving an angry email? Would you be offended by that email, left feeling disenfranchised or unmotivated? The Golden Rule applies to every aspect of email communication.

3. <u>**Check your mood.**</u> As you begin to compose that email, make a quick assessment of what mood you're in because *that* mood is going to translate itself into your email. Are you crabby? Disinterested? Are you frustrated? Irritable? Somewhere in that email, your mood will sift through. Better to wait until you're upbeat and pleasant and can come from a positive attitude before sending *any* email, even if it's one where you're rightfully complaining or taking issue with something or someone. (I've learned this the hard way!) For example, there was the time I wrote an email to a PR client who had been very dishonest with me and my staff, telling him that we felt it necessary to notify him immediately that we could no longer represent him. When I terminated him I should have just written, "We regret having to terminate our services, but we find it necessary." Instead, I added, "And I certainly don't think I need to explain why." That had the unfortunate effect of making him angry and in the mood to retaliate with a lot of unnecessary email dissing.

4. <u>**Check your tone.**</u> The old saying about "reading between the lines" could not be more accurate when it comes to email. If your words are saying one thing, but the tone in your underlying voice is screaming something else, go back to the keyboard and start over. A series of emails that demonstrate a negative subtext could mean the loss of a client or customer. All of us in business need to keep our relationships intact.

5. **Be consistent.** Most of us are creatures of habit. If we consistently send emails that transmit the same ol' sour disposition, people won't want to hear from us. Instead, if we always throw some humor into the email message mix, they will look forward to clicking and reading. The habits you have established with word choices and mood preferences will perpetuate themselves. Decide what type of countenance best characterizes your email persona. Don't be all over the map. Don't send a scathing email one day and a sugary sweet one the next. (I once had a bi-polar emailer for a client. Wow, he gave a whole new meaning to the term "mood swing"!) You need consistency in your communication and so does the audience of customers with whom you interact. Make sure your expression is always a positive and pleasant one, consistently professional.

6. **Slow down.** I'm sure you will balk at this rule, but you must take the time to do a quick run-through of EVERY email before you send it to make sure your words are well-chosen and fit together well. Not taking enough time is what gets a lot of us into trouble. I've said it a dozen times and I'll say it again: good communication in any form is all about making the human connection and building rapport. If there is no connection, there will be a "diss" connection. If we don't have rapport, we have nothing.

If you rely on email as the vehicle to conduct your business affairs, practice the rules above religiously. In the end, you will save yourself a lot of grief. You will also make the appropriate impression each and every time you send an email and strengthen your business relationships.

I've stated from the outset of this book that one of the major problems as email addicts is that we use email much of the time to do the talking for us. The trick then is to recognize what it is you are *really* saying and to make sure that your message is said with dignity, class and consideration for the person who is receiving it.

HE SAID, SHE SAID...

For further clarification and for your entertainment pleasure, I offer the following before-and-after emails, culled from homework assignments turned in by students. I'm hopeful that they will help you further distinguish nice from naughty.

Naughty:
"...*I'm simply too busy to look it up right now. You'll have to wait.*"

Ouch! Grab me a band-aid! Note that the use of the word "simply" in this context sounds, well, downright snotty. It needs to be deleted. The phrase, "You'll have to wait," is very "diss"missive and the person receiving this email couldn't help but feel put down. The underlying subtext is condescending, to say the least.

You may think that people don't really send such emails, but you're wrong. They do. Now, if you were to *say* those same two phrases aloud, attaching a different mood to them, as my improv actors or ExecuProv students studying "self-expression" are taught to do, you might say them in a way that is anything but condescending or angry. Unfortunately, your recipient *can't hear* you deliver those two phrases. They only see the words on the screen. They will give them their own subjective interpretation.

Let's say the actor or speaker delivers the above mentioned two phrases in a state of rushed excitement. That would make those lines fun, wouldn't it? Go ahead, try it! Or, if they said them with an attitude of begging desperation, they would not sound offensive, they might even elicit sympathy. But all bets are off when your vocalization is absent because you are writing. You only have words to get your tone across. So again, choose your words wisely and make sure their underlying intent is one that will create a bond with the other person, not a falling out.

Here's an "after" version of the email above, using words chosen to get the message across without rancor, impatience or snippiness.

Nice:
"…*wish I could look it up right now but I'm jammed. Wait. Please bear with me!*"

Very different *feel,* yes? The tone in the email redo conveys a whole different message than the earlier version.

Here we go with another email. The focus here is on the subtext.

Naughty:
"*I will try to be at the 9 a.m. meeting if my schedule lets up. I've got a workload that isn't mine, but I know it has to get done.*"

Oh, somebody please get a Kleenex! Poor pitiful emailer. Though he doesn't come out and say it, the subtext screams "poor me!" Beneath that is a whole lot of resentment. The boss who received that email will either feel guilty or become irritated that his employee is whining about getting the job done. There are other more effective ways to get the point across. Deleting the word "try" would be helpful. Substituting "allows" for "lets up," would also take the foot off the resentment pedal. The second sentence is loaded with martyrdom and I doubt that this passive-aggressive approach will motivate the boss to jump in and take some of the unfair burden off his employee.
Here's a second take on the same email:

Nice:
"I'll be at the 9 a.m. meeting if I get on top of this workload. If you can reassign some of it to someone else, I sure would appreciate it. Any chance?"

If you really want to inspire the boss to help out, better to come at him with an honest appeal rather than to alienate him with whining.

Here are a few more before-and-after emails, without explanations. I think you'll get the picture.

Naughty:
"You always seem to ask me the same question. Didn't I already answer that?"
(Oooh. That's going to leave a psychological mark!)

Nice:
"Oops. Guess I wasn't communicating adequately to satisfy your question. Here it is one more time, a bit more clearly, I hope."

Naughty:
"Forward me the Mendez file and I mean now."
(Help! Someone call the email ambulance!)

Nice:
"Need the Mendez file, like now! Oh, please!"

For fun and to strengthen your email composition chops, take ten emails that you've either received or sent this week that might fall within the "naughty" category. Now, redo them nicely. If you want to get really creative, try five or six redo's of the same naughty email and note how many wonderful choices you have at your expressive fingertips! I had one client who got so enthused about this exercise that he staged a contest within his office. He sent out a naughty email that read: *"I told you not to attach the mission statement. I told you to cut and paste it. Why can't you follow simple directions?"* The winner's redo said: *"Mission statement: Paste. Cut. Third grade concept, yes, but it's the only way I can get it! Thanks, your email playground buddy."* He got a plasma big screen. Gee, wish I worked for him. I do something creative and all I get is a piece of chocolate. (But then I work for myself!)

HUMOR THEM

The winner of the "mission statement" email contest was on the right track, I think, for humor is very bonding and tends to lighten anyone's email load. His redo message was direct in terms of word choices. He explicitly expressed his need, and the tone—I thought it was a fun one. His humorous approach did not offend. It motivated.

When I teach my one-on-one communication skills classes, I always tell my students to give others what they need and want so *they* can get what they want and need. If the winning email had been sent to the target recipient with that humorous touch, there would have been a better vibe between the emailer and the receiver.

For another homework assignment try taking that terse and laconic message you're about to send and giving it a humorous spin. For example, rather than saying "Bring donuts," maybe you can say, "Will sing for donuts." You may be pleasantly surprised at how good you make the other person feel when they receive it. The way to measure your success is in your return email responses. What's the vibe like? Good, bad? Cold, warm? You'll know when you've hit the mark.

I don't know about you, but I get upward of a hundred emails daily. I spend a good part of my day on the computer answering them. I cannot tell you how many times I have had a sense of comic workplace relief when opening a humorously crafted email. It makes my day! How about you? Naturally, you don't want to use sarcasm or comic jabs at anyone's expense. Always put the joke on yourself, or on the Universe, or on the problem at hand. I am certain this approach will get you the good vibe you're after.

In two of my books, *Funny Business: How to Make* <u>You</u> *Laugh on the Job Every Day,* and *What's So Funny? How To Get Humor and Good Storytelling into your Speeches and Presentations,* I have guidelines that better define the how-to's of using humor. You might want to pick up a copy of each or go online and see what else Amazon.com or Google may have in book form to help you learn how to insert humor into your communications.

MISCELLANEOUS WHATNOTS

There are a few final rules that I would like to pass on to you here that can strongly affect whether your email is perceived as "naughty or nice." What they have in common is that they represent email pitfalls that you've probably never even thought of:

1. **<u>Bone up on global customs.</u>** Though I don't do work internationally, many of the business people I know do. It seems that what might be acceptable email parlance in the United States may actually offend someone in a foreign land. For instance, writing "Hi John" to an executive in the U.S. is perfectly acceptable. However, saying anything but "Dear Mr. Smith" to an executive in, let's say, China might be construed as a "naughty" gesture — a sign of disrespect.

2. **<u>All caps?</u>** Some say that sending emails with each word in capital letters is a capitol offense! When I send an email to my sister that says, "HOW ARE YOU?" she says I'm yelling at her. She finds that naughty! I certainly didn't intend to be! Going back to what I said earlier, it is best to check with your email recipients, find out their preferences, and try

to fulfill their expectations. I'm sure your goal is to always make nice! What may be naughty or nice in some workplace circles may differ from others.

3. **Subject lines.** Rick Rhoads, one of the most top-notch marketing and communication experts I've ever met, says that what you put in a subject line is equivalent to a "headline" (the line that appears above an advertisement). He says it helps the recipient know whether they should read your email now or later, and where to file the message so that they can locate it when they are searching for it two weeks later. Having a descriptive subject line also helps you to quickly find your message in your "sent" folder. (And how many of us have had to frantically sift through a hundred messages trying to figure out what we said to a client that got *that* response!) Writing "Re: Something" or "From John" in the subject is too vague. As an example of an unambiguous email subject line, Rhoads cites the following from a message he wrote to a client: "11 Early Signs," the beginning of the title of an article he was writing for the client. When he needed more information the next morning, he changed the subject line to read: "11 Early Signs; need more info today." He also asserts that it is polite to send an entire message in the subject line. For instance, Rhoads says you can easily put "Yes on lunch 11/4 12 noon Juniors NM." The "NM=no message." He says that's just good etiquette and saves the recipient valuable time.

Another note from Rhoads: If you receive an email that appropriately copies several other recipients, hitting the "reply to all" button is appropriate. However, out of habit, many people only hit the "reply" button, inadvertently cutting everyone but the original sender out of the loop. Oops, I've been naughty like that more than once! How about you? Again, be nice.

4. **Watch how you word messages**. There are times when being naughty can get you in more trouble than you bargained for. I have many lawyer clients and friends who cannot stress enough how important it is to be careful what you say and how you say it in your emails. When you decide to be naughty in an email, you must ask yourself, "Could this be used against me in a court of law?" Suits happen! And email is often an issue.

5. **Oh that shorthand!** Not everyone knows "LOL" (laughing out loud, they may confuse it with lots of luck), "BTW" (by the way) or, my favorite, "RME" (rolling my eyes). Since there is no actual shorthand handbook for email yet, make sure the people with whom you correspond on the email front "get" your acronym lingo.

6. **Personal touch**. Find out whether your company policy allows for sending emails of a personal nature from your workplace computer. Many experts say you ought not to use the company time or equipment to send naughty or nice email messages to friends and family while on the job. I know people who have sent a "naughty" email to an ex-lover telling them how they planned to effect their revenge, thus putting their employer at risk. Then there are those "nice" emails to a lover describing what they most enjoyed about the "night before." Since everything you write from a networked office computer gets saved, that could be embarrassing!

7. **Disclaimer**. If you want to protect the privacy of your outgoing emails, put a permanent disclaimer at the bottom under your signature information. There

are many people in the workplace who will not respect your privacy unless they know they may be committing a criminal act (this is so, I am told, within the legal community) or that they may get sued in civil court for sharing your email communication. For example, the disclaimer that automatically appears at the close of every email I send through my company states: *The information contained in this communication from Kerr Companies and ExecuProv is confidential material and is intended for the designated recipient only with the exception of attachments meant for, and specified for, wide distribution to the media. If you are not the intended recipient, you are hereby advised that any disclosure, copying, distribution or use of the contents of this email is prohibited. If you received this communication in error, please notify us immediately by email and delete the original message.* Including a disclaimer, if you feel your company needs one, may protect your privacy and give you a sense of security and peace of mind. As I have pointed out all along in this book, there are no real hard and fast rules about email, and the laws necessary for protecting those who use the cyber highways are trailing far behind the need for them. A disclaimer may not protect you completely, but it does serve as a deterrent; so, you can protect yourself to some extent. Conversely, you should always respect the disclaimers you see at the end of others' emails. The last thing you want to risk is a lawsuit! Besides, respecting someone else's privacy is the decent thing to do.

FINAL THOUGHTS

One of your assignments in this chapter was to go back and read your emails to discern whether they were naughty or nice, and rewrite them. Now do what my students do:

Take some of those emails that made you feel uncomfortable, angry or hurt and test your email prowess by redoing those, too. Soon you'll have a very clear understanding of what will garner a positive vibe, and what will not. You'll also know right from wrong.

Use this admonishment as your yardstick: With my email, am I being naughty or making nice?

"You don't look anything like your emails!"

Chapter Seven

UP OR DOWN?
Feeling high; gettin' low.

As I was asking myself and others to whom I had posed the same question about what we all hated about email, I came to realize that one of the things most of us email addicts dislike are the highs and lows. All of us have days when email can actually alter our mood—for good or bad.

Since "getting clean" and email withdrawal are not options for most of us, we have to learn to work with it, through it and in spite of it. Liken the ups and downs of email reactions, if you will, to those of the hardcore junkie on drugs. It's difficult to sustain a moderate high—to level off and keep the buzz steady. While your drug of choice— email—brings you moments when you feel terrific "on it," and you're on it much of the time, you will undoubtedly have your share of times when it will make you feel crummy.

Granted, there are many days when the emails we get are innocuous and uneventful, just business as usual. But when we are on the receiving end of an upsetting email, our buttons can, and do, get pushed. We can suffer a hangover from these experiences for days.

In the last chapter we covered how certain word choices and subtext can make us and others feel. We explored *why* our buttons get pushed. Now it's time to lay out some clear-cut rules for *how* we can stop that from happening in order to stave off the email blues.

STAYING POWER

Emails that evoke a negative emotion in us are difficult to manage. For instance, what about that boss or customer who is making constant demands or flinging criticisms at you in their missives all day long? I doubt that those same people stop intermittently to thank or compliment you to help balance out your psyche. No, many emails are sent because things have to get done, problems arise and fires have to be put out. A sender taking care of his or her pressing issues is not focusing on diplomacy. Nevertheless, a series of disturbing emails can cause our otherwise enthusiastic approach to our workday to plummet, resulting in moods that shift dramatically. Well, you might ask, doesn't communication by phone or in person give you the same highs and lows as email communication? Sure, for most of us, but here's where I think the situation differs: negative email communication cuts deeper because the impact of words on your computer screen lasts longer. I know business colleagues who have sat and stared at the face of their desk or laptop reading and rereading an email message for hours, then continued to obsess over it throughout the day to the point of distraction and ultimate debilitation.

I always tell my P.R. clients that what they hear will vanish far more quickly from memory than what they read in print. Print just seems so indelible. You can have a piece of communication on the phone or in a meeting that isn't all that pleasant and the memory of it will dissipate. However, when something is in writing, whether paper or computer screen, it lingers. It is more penetrable and enduring. For one thing, when people are stung by an email, they are tempted to go back and reread it. Conversely, if someone throws a verbal insult your way, they don't keep repeating it. You only hear it once. With email, the less-than-pleasant message can be replayed over and over again if you don't have the discipline to let it go. I'm told by my focus groups that when negative emails come to them, they do read them more than once. Each time an email is re-read it serves to kick off the reader's negative reaction to it from scratch. The miserable cycle starts all over again. I know people who have re-read emails for weeks.

DISS YOU!

Tracy Gibbs, a pharmaceutical salesperson, told me about one particular email that put her into a deep funk. It was the afternoon her boss told her in an abrupt email someone else was going to assume her sales territory and she would have to transfer to another region. "The way it was worded made me feel so insignificant. Especially when I emailed back to ask why and he wouldn't answer me," Gibbs confided. "I walked around with the same feeling of discomfort you get when you've had a bad dream and can't shake it." The "diss" of it all stayed with her for a long time, she said. It wasn't the reassignment of territory, because she preferred the new one over the old. It was the way he chose to "notify" her. As an independent sales rep, she even thought about going without email so that those in her work world would have to contact her personally and directly, but she, like the rest of us, knows that once you're hooked on email, it's hard to kick the habit. Still, her boss's email had left its psychological mark on her.

Kate Braniff of PAN Communications told me she viewed email from a similar vantage point. She said that when she sent emails that no one responded to, it reminded her of that same horrible pit-of-your-stomach feeling of rejection you experience while waiting for a guy to return your phone call — and he never does.

As an email society we need to deal with issues like these.

HIGH AND LOW

As I began to further investigate the high/low aspects of email and how they could make business professionals *feel*, I was amazed to learn that, for those I queried, there wasn't a day that went by in which they hadn't suffered some hurt, annoyance or disappointment because of what had popped up on their email screens. The majority of them also told me they had no clue as to how to mitigate the negative feelings they experienced as a result of these thoughtless missives. It wasn't always the content of the message or the information it contained, they said. It was the way the email was presented. Yes, I know, I would tell them. I get them, too and they can powerfully disturb our equilibrium. Someone barking an order such as "Get coffee to the conference room by 10 and do not be late with it," may seem to the sender like a rushed request, harmless from their viewpoint. But click open enough of those kinds of emails over an hour or two, and you can begin to feel pretty demoralized.

LET ME OUT, LET ME IN

I asked the handful of groups who provided feedback to me on this front how much time they spend online each day. Most said the majority of their workday. Some said it was their only means of connecting to people all day.

This brings me to my next point about how email can make us feel: isolated and detached.

A student spoke up in my workshop one day to say that on many workdays he felt as if he'd been relegated to "solitary confinement." At first we laughed at the analogy, but then when we began to discuss it, we realized it wasn't all that funny! When this guy used the word "removed" to describe how he experienced his interactions with those in the workplace, the rest of the group bobbed their heads in the affirmative.

I found his description interesting. So did the rest of the class. We could relate to it.

I certainly knew what he meant, for even though I had been in contact with people via email all day some days, somehow, I too, felt unusually alone. This seemed oddly ironic to me since I'm not one to *need* people a lot. I'm very independent and I really enjoy my solitude. But since my students kept bringing it up, I felt that the isolation issue was yet another area that needed to be addressed, one more important item in the email etiquette equation.

CHARTING THE COURSE

I asked my workshop attendees to start keeping a journal about how many email highs and lows they had in one business day, tally up their answers for a week, then email me the results. Sure enough, the ratio was about ten to one, one being the "up" email moments. Only a few of the emails received were viewed as "business as usual" — those that didn't leave a negative emotional or psychological impression.

Some of those I asked to journal told me that their highs when they received strongly positive emails were somewhat over the top because they weren't used to someone taking the time to show them appreciation or kindness. While they were very glad to get these kinds of messages, for the most part, almost everyone said that by the end of the business day, their nerves were frayed from incoming messages that were demanding, critical and oft times downright demeaning. Most told me that they carried the residue from weighty emails long after they had arrived home and would continue to obsess over them. I'd had many a day and evening ruined, too, because of email, so I knew how they felt.

For those of us who conduct a good part of our business activities by email, it can be hard to endure these ups and downs forty hours a week. But then, once again, what to do about them? That's an important question.

I decided that there had to be rules for keeping even-keeled, but these rules would have to be self-imposed and we would have to stay on top of ourselves to make them stick. My goal then would be to create a set of precepts that would help us remain cheerful and upbeat as we went about our work tasks, despite the nature of some of our email correspondence. Yes, it was all about keeping our spirits up and preventing email from dominating our moods.

SOME OF MY FAVORITE THINGS

Interestingly, this chapter is the most important one to me because I despise those days when I feel as if I've been dissed-out and yanked in every emotional direction. I also feel pretty glum after a long day of sensing I've been sequestered from humankind, i.e., it's not me and other guy, it's me and the computer.

Without getting mired in psycho-babble, I do want to point out that I truly believe we all need to take responsibility for our feelings, or at least do something about them when someone stirs them in a negative way. Maybe we can't change the email habits of others, but we can certainly change ourselves, our perspective and our reactions to them.

With this goal in mind, I've devised the *Bliss or "Diss"* 12-Step program. Its rules should be followed just like the ones in previous chapters—choose the ones that work for you. These rules are all designed to take good care of *you* no matter what is going on in the email scheme of things. Here are my ideas:

1. **Don't deny**—that you've just been dissed by an email. Upon reading a message with a negative tone, take stock of your physical and emotional

symptoms. Is your pulse racing, the pace of your breath quickening, your brow scrunching, your shoulders slumping? Did you go from a feeling of "Can't wait to get the job tasks of the day done," to "I just want to go home"? Face email reality. Awareness is the first step in doing something positive to combat the email doldrums. Unfortunately, most people just ignore their symptoms. Then one day they go postal! So, if someone sends you an email that says, "Talk to you next week. I have really important stuff to get to today," recognize that you've just been dissed.

2. **Clarify**—the message or state your case. Let's say the above-mentioned email comes your way. Rather than just ignoring it you can always write back with an appropriate response. It can be anything from "Did you say next week? If so, please provide day and time to talk. Would appreciate it," to "But this *is* important. We need to talk sooner than next week. Like today." Often we get bent out of shape because of the subtext ("I have really important stuff to get to today," which infers that the recipient is not important). Nailing down a specific time to deal with an issue, or asserting yourself by saying it is important *now*, regardless of whether or not the person responds according to your wishes, is a way of letting them know, in subtext, that you're holding your own. You'll feel better about yourself for not wilting or brooding, and if you approach the email perpetrator appropriately he or she will come to respect you.

3. **Take a break**—to shake off the negative email vibe. This may mean stepping away from the

computer to take a restroom break, getting a cup of coffee from the lunchroom, or making a phone call to someone who is always glad to hear your voice. Me? I reapply my lipstick or read the AOL Headlines before taking to my email duties again.

4. **Don't take it personally**—because the person on the other end may have his or her own issues, none of which have anything to do with you. If you did nothing to provoke a negative email vibe, get a grip. Their "diss" missive stance may be a result of their insecurities or troubles. Don't let them project those onto you. Have a nice day!

5. **Confront the email perpetrator**—in an appropriate way. Don't get defensive, argumentative (remember the rules in Chapter One) or attack. Let the person know that what they have said bothers you. For instance, an apt response to the email above may be, "Perhaps you didn't mean it this way, but your last email makes me feel as though I am not important. I believe that I am and that this is subject matter we need to discuss and soon. I thought it necessary to be upfront with you about it." You just may be pleasantly surprised at the response. If you don't receive an apology, know that you have expressed your "diss" content in a kind and direct manner. No one can argue with that and you're left feeling whole and dignified. Many people let such an email slide and, well, can you say "resentment" with a capital "R?" That's what may build up over time.

6. **Make an appeal**—to the person who sent you the email. One way to handle the aforementioned email is to tell them that you realize they are

busy and have important things to tend to, but you truly need their help, and right away. Sometimes an honest and open response can change the email climate entirely. I always think this approach is worth a try.

7. **Plan a strategy** — that you can put into play when you receive an email that disappoints, frustrates or irritates you. For instance, one of my students prints out the negative emails he receives for a week (the ones that clearly illustrate the "diss" connection), and without using names, posts them on a nom de plume MySpace page. "These are this week's sampling of emails that should never have been sent," it starts. For him, this is a way to vent. I have another student who prints out his "worst" email of the day and posts it in the lunchroom. Then he and his small staff use the email *du jour* regularly for target practice as a way to sharpen their dart game. Whatever makes you feel better without hurting someone else in the process is what you should think about when planning a strategy to make yourself feel better. Make it an easy one that you can put into play right away. I have yet another student who keeps a joke book on his desk. Whenever he gets an email that disturbs his good mood, he swings around in his chair, grabs the book and reads for a minute or two. He claims this helps him to "equalize" his mood.

8. **Delete** — the email from your mailbox unless you need it for some important reason. You don't want to be tempted to read it a second time nor do you want it contaminating your "good" mail. Any email that is blatantly rude, insulting or demeaning belongs in the trash. Put it there.

9. **Ply a little humor**—because it makes everyone feel better. This is my favorite of all the rules. Nothing helps a bad mood dissipate faster than a little laughter. Send a humorous email in response to the one that put you off. However, be careful not to be biting, caustic, sarcastic or demeaning to the person to whom you're sending it. Putting the joke on yourself always works. If you had been the recipient of "Talk to you next week. I have really important stuff to get to today," how about cutting and pasting that message and sending something in return that he/she might never expect, like "But wait: I want to be part of that stuff!" Humor, done appropriately, can be the most positive approach to any negative communication situation. It diffuses anger, allows people to see things from a different perspective, and provides the opportunity to start the communication from scratch on a positive note. Done right, there is nothing more bonding than humor!

10. **Reward yourself**—for not stooping to someone's level of "diss" courtesy. Though it's tempting to offer tit for email-tat, don't. Congratulate yourself for keeping your cool and a sense of class. The goal is to boost your self-esteem, not diminish it. So, give yourself credit and a reward when you're good. Download a new iTune, throw an extra scoop of whipped cream on that latte, or stop on the way home and take in a movie you've been dying to see.

11. **Spread some good cheer**—to others. Nothing feels better than turning your back on a negative email and composing a positive one to a work colleague you've been meaning to contact. Ask how they're doing. Let them know they are

appreciated. See what they're up to. Chances are, they will respond with a kind message of their own. That's sure something you could use to balance out the day!

12. **Stay connected** — to your core values as a respectable emailer. Though you may have one of those days when you almost don't care what you say in an email because you're so fed up with ones you've been getting, don't succumb. You don't want to hate yourself when you clock out at the end of the day still ruminating over the emails you sent — the ones that lacked good manners, sensitivity and kindness. Part of the personal responsibility you should assume when getting behind the keyboard and driving the cyber highways is to email according to the road signs (etiquette) spelled out in each of the *Bliss or "Diss"* chapters.

In terms of the isolation issue, if you have become somewhat reclusive, force yourself to socialize. This could mean making several telephone calls instead of the email responses that seem so much more convenient, or making a little chit-chat with co-workers. If you sit behind your computer most of the day or communicate via BlackBerry, show up at the next chamber mixer luncheon and shake a few hands. We all need a little live company throughout the day. No man is an email island!

FEEL FOR THE OTHER GUY

Perhaps it goes without saying, but there are several rules for just plain good manners when it comes to being considerate of the other guy's feelings — how you affect his/her ups and downs. I include my "Top Ten" absolutes as to what I think should be incorporated into the HR manual under the "email etiquette" tab. Taking some responsibility for someone *else's* sensitivities and what makes them feel insignificant or uncomfortable is all part of the package. Most of these rules have to do with common sense, you might say, but take a look around. Just about everyone I know violates these rules at least once a day:

PLEASE **DO NOT:**

1. <u>Glance at your PDA incessantly or at all during a meeting</u>—whether you are sitting with one person or several. It's best to turn it off so that you're not tempted to "diss"connect while in the presence of others. If you don't do this, you might as well walk into the room, sit down and announce, "I'm far more important to myself than any of you are." Refresh your memory by revisiting Rule #7 in Chapter Two and the concept of "Attending to." Nothing personifies "rude" more than constantly checking your PDA while you are supposed to be participating fully in a meeting. Remember, these are your colleagues or customers—people with whom you are expected to be interacting and toward whom you need to be respectful.

2. <u>Talk on the phone while reading or typing emails</u>—because you can't possibly focus on the person at the other end of line if you are preoccupied with something else. Think "single-tasking" instead of multi-tasking. Whenever I hear someone typing away while I'm carrying on a conversation with them, it not only makes me feel insignificant, but also angry. You, too, can probably feel the "diss" connect when you suddenly realize that the person with whom you're having a telephone conversation is engaged in sending email messages to someone

other than you. Most business professionals are not good enough actors to fake you out. They give themselves away with a series of distracted comments such as "Oh, uh-huh," "Yes," "Uh-huh…"

3. **Take your PDA to a formal presentation**— because it's just too tempting to pull it out and check your messages, or send them, while someone else is attempting to educate, inform or make a pitch to you. They have center stage. Show them the same respect you would want if you were in their workplace shoes.

4. **Leave your PDA in your briefcase or on the desk where it is constantly ringing and pinging**—it is bound to annoy someone unless your office is soundproof. Even if this were the case, let's say that someone calls you on a LAND-line and while you are engaged in a conversation with them, they can hear the PDA background noise. You might as well announce, "I'll be listening to you for only part of the time."

5. **Cut off your dialogue or that of someone's else when your PDA notifies you of an incoming email or cell phone call**—unless you first excuse yourself or ask permission to check the incoming message. I have heard many people curtly interrupt the person with whom they are speaking, even in mid-sentence (!) by saying, "I have to take this." Most of the time they turn their backs to you and don't even say "sorry." You *don't* have to take it. Let the person know, nicely, that this is not acceptable.

6. **When in the presence of strangers or others**—in elevators, on subway platforms or bus benches,

in office supply stores and in other locations, don't start checking and sending email messages (or chattering away on your cell phone). When human beings are present, we should make an effort to exchange pleasantries, strike up conversations or show simple kindnesses, such as saying, "Can I get that for you?" or "How are *you* doing today?" Unfortunately, you see many people use these workday "lags" as a means to further "diss" humanity and isolate themselves. Do you know that networking can happen virtually anywhere?

7. <u>**Take your PDA to the company party**</u>—You may laugh, but there are people who do this. I find nothing more pretentious or obnoxious than seeing a partygoer whip out their PDA to answer an email or shoot one off. PDAs do not belong at social functions. Tuck yours away. You are there to socialize, not "diss"-alize!

8. <u>**Read and send emails while driving**</u>—or operating heavy machinery! This is not just for your safety and the safety of others around you. You can easily make an email mistake if your attention isn't focused on what you are doing. I once had an employee say in a rushed email to a potential client, "We are an award-winning *pubic* relations firm." Pull over or flip the "off" lever on the mega-shredder and take a time out.

9. <u>**Take your PDA to a company class, seminar or workshop**</u>—leave yours in the car. Typically, there are others in your class who don't appreciate the interruptions your PDA causes. In ExecuProv classes, all students are required to turn off their devices and put them in a basket until break or

until class is dismissed. I threaten my students with a ruler to the knuckles. (Just kidding!)

10. **Take your PDA to the company restroom** — because others may be using the facilities as well, and nothing says "I'm classless" more blatantly! Also, I have known more than one person who had to make a frantic last-minute decision as to whether to retrieve the accidentally dropped device or allow it to be flushed away! Talk about crisis management!

IN SUMMARY

While I think all the guidelines I've put forth in the book are extremely important, the ones I've just covered could prove to be the most important of all. And one more thing, don't send personal emails from work. It is not only disrespectful to your employer; it can get you into trouble.

I believe that if each of us takes really good care of ourselves and others as we go about using email communication effectively, we will maximize our relationships. If you can establish and maintain really meaningful business relationships, you cannot help but be successful. In the end, I think that's all any of us wants — to be triumphant in whatever field we choose.

I will round out this chapter with an interesting concept for your consideration. Earlier in the book I talked about many of the tenets we learn as improv comedy players and how they so appropriately apply to everyday communication. Here's another: as we develop improvised scenes we don't focus so much on the "what" in the scene, that is, the set-up (situation) the audience has assigned us, for instance, a couple in the midst of purchasing a car at a dealership. Instead, the actors place their emphasis more on the "who" and the "why" in order to bring the piece to the human level. For example, for the "who," one set of improv artists created the scenario that they were a couple of transients who had pooled their money to buy a car. "Why," they needed one was because they had to get to L.A. to audition for a film about the homeless. This makes the scene much richer and more interesting to the audience. Now, if we could just take that same precept and apply it to our email communications so that we could get more into the "*who*" and "*why*," and not so much into the "*what*," we would create far more interesting and "connectable" emails.

As I mentioned earlier in the book, I have been in the communications field since the 70s and though technology has constantly changed, I do not believe that people's need to be become more connected to one another and to stay that way has changed at all. With that in mind, I strongly urge you to take the *Bliss or "Diss"* rules to heart and use them throughout every day.

Let's move forward now for a quick peek at what some people say may trump email, further advancing technology in terms of how people will communicate with one another in the not-too-distant future.

"This meeting will now come to order."

Epilogue

IN OR OUT?
What's next, what's new?

I hope the chapters in this book have provided insights into the email phenomenon from a perspective you had not considered before. In this etiquette manual, I have stressed the importance of presenting yourself more professionally through your email communications, offered strategies for how to use email to establish, build and maintain meaningful and solid business relationships, and suggested guidelines for how to make the human connection with others, well, more *connectable.*

I do not think any of us business professionals are going to kick the addiction to technology. In fact, as it continues to offer us new advances in communicating with one another electronically, I think the good majority of us will remain perpetually strung out!

I'm not suggesting that's a bad thing. Surely, as we've evolved through time, we've become fully dependent on other revolutionary and labor-saving devices. Take the telephone, for instance. How about the automobile? Or my favorite, the microwave. What intrigues me, however, is what's next. What is just around the corner that will eventually replace email as *the* means of communicating with one another in the workplace.

Just for fun (because I'm big on that), I always wind up my email classes by asking my students what they predict will come along to replace email. With that closer, many drop their jaws, scrunch their brows and scratch their heads as they try to consider what the heck that might be. I get a lot of *Star Trek* stuff. Then there are always some who get that pained looked on their faces, mortified at the thought of email disappearing. I try to assuage their fears by telling them that just like the telephone, email won't become extinct, but clearly there will be something that will supersede or expand it.

Then the fun begins.

Some of the comments below are from my students, but I also asked a broad cross-section of people of all ages to weigh in with answers to the same question: what's next? The following are some of their ideas, suggestions and, more importantly, their beliefs about what the future holds with respect to how we will be communicating with one another in the future.

Paul Miller, a vice president for Marketfare Foods, says, "I think we're headed for communication through mental telepathy and that eventually we will all become more mechanical than biological. I think you'll be able to program your mind to pick up and send communication by projecting it over telepathic waves. I see each of us having thought spammers to filter out incoming messages we don't want. So, I'm going to predict 'E-Telepathy.'" When I asked Miller, who is incredibly silly and fun, if that meant we would also be able to block people's thoughts he enthused, "Yes, especially your ex, a disgruntled former employee or the no-show vendor who's begging to get back into your good graces."

Ten-year-old Natalie from southern California said that if it were up to her she would invent glasses that enabled you to see the person with whom you wished to communicate.

After that, she went off into a *Mission Impossible* scenario, but I was lost in thought wondering how that would affect my contact lenses.

Ben, an ardent ExecuProv student and an erudite type, said he thought we would be signing up at out-patient clinics by the dozens to have a chip implanted in the earlobe of choice. "You'll just press the lobe, speak, press it again and off goes the message." When others in class and I asked him how he would receive and print out communication (just as you do email from a computer), he confidently asserted, "Oh, that's easy. You just hook up to a lobe scanner which is attached to a multi-quick laser printer—a miniature one that you can carry in your briefcase or purse—and out it comes." A little far-fetched, perhaps, but the class burst into applause in a show of support.

One of my assistants at work came up with the idea of an advanced remote control device that would send email from your flat screen television set and your GPS system in your car. She was trying to describe to me how this hypothetical technology operated and how it differed from existing text messaging and remote control devices via charades, acting out pushing the buttons on what I guess was the command system. But, since I still can't even work the remote that operates my cable TV system, I could only feign understanding by nodding appreciatively.

My son-in-law, who is one of the sharpest guys I know, said, "Oh, email replacement? That's simple. Eventually, we won't even have computers. Everything will be communicated via some type of Bluetooth device and monitored by a GPS System. Not only will we be able to send and receive what was once email communication, we'll be able to open our locked file drawers, regulate the office thermostat, and pour a cup of coffee with a simple voice command into our Bluetooth." When I asked him what he thought about us wearing a small headset permanently, he quickly corrected me, "No. No headset. We'll have some type of chip, surgically implanted behind the ear."

He was on the same page as Ben.

While some of these may sound outlandish, don't forget Marconi and the radio, Farnsworth, Zworykin and Baird, the inventers of television, Bain and the fax machine, and the often overlooked Strite and the advent of the pop-up toaster. While Strite's invention certainly makes breakfast more fun, the others literally created communication devices that seemed to send and receive their messages through "thin air."

Do not be afraid that your beloved email will disappear overnight. When it comes to transmitting information from one source to another, do not discount how many steps of evolution it took to get to where we are today and how many more it will take before we get that chip implant! But if all of this sounds implausible, simply take a step back in history and look at how far we've come in communicating with others. It all started with the forefathers of communication—the pharaohs who sent their ideas and messages via hieroglyphics. Many improvements in writing down messages followed, of course, but finally came Samuel Finley Breese Morse and his Morse code. Thankfully, his ingenuity kicked off the telegram. Then not that very long ago, Ray Tomlinson and his TENEX system led to the ARPANET (all Greek to me!), the Big Daddy of email.

As you finish the final page of this book you can be sure someone somewhere right now is concocting a new device for communicating a message from one person to another that will (sooner than we think) replace the system we now know as email. Whatever it is, I only hope that person does not forget to include a book of etiquette, one that emphasizes how important it will always be to create the human and business connection in ways that emphasize "relationship."

If I had my way I would invent a device that transcribed and transmitted a person's message in a flash, but edited and revised it automatically according to a person's personality on their best day.

How about you?

ABOUT THE AUTHOR

Cherie Kerr founded ExecuProv in 1983, and has provided a variety of classes on presentation and communication skills to hundreds of business professionals from Fortune 500 companies ever since. Her clients include Ericsson, Toyota, Kawasaki, Mitsubishi, Ingram Micro, Bank One, Delta Dental, Experian, Foothill Capital, PacifiCare, Allergan, Universal Studios, Fluor Corporation, 3i Implant, ConAgra Foods, The Hilton Hotel and Marriott Hotel Corporations, California Trucking Association, Office Max/Boise, Office Depot and the U.S. Naval Academy at Annapolis, to name but a few. She also has worked for a number of governmental agencies including the L.A. City Attorney's Office, the L.A. District Attorney's office, the County of Orange, the Orange County Bar Foundation and the Orange County Juvenile Drug Court Program. She is a certified Provider for the Continuing Legal Education Program for the State Bar of California, and has served as that organization's official speaker-trainer for its Board of Governors.

A founding member of the world-famous L.A. Groundlings, Kerr was the founder in 1990, Executive Producer and Artistic Director for the Orange County Crazies, a sketch and improvisational comedy troupe in Santa Ana, California. She also served as the group's head writer. She has received rave reviews for her work as a writer, performer and director.

Kerr has taught improvisational comedy to actors for the past 30 years, and teaches other classes as well, including a class on how to develop original characters and how to write sketch comedy. She has studied with some of the best improv and comedy teachers in the business, including Gary Austin, founder of the L.A. Groundlings, and a former member of the highly acclaimed group, The Committee, Michael Gellman, a director and teacher for Second City, in Chicago, and Jeannie Berlin (an Academy Award nominee and Elaine May's daughter.) In her formative years, she studied at the Pasadena Academy of Drama with Eleanor Dopp.

A writer for more than 30 years, Kerr has owned an award-winning public relations firm and still works as a consultant in that field. She has written, produced and directed an original full-scale musical comedy, is a member of ASCAP, and has been honored as an award-winning journalist and publicist. Kerr was named, along with Disney's Michael Eisner, as one of the "Top Ten Most Sensational People in Orange County" by *Orange Coast Magazine*. She has been quoted and featured in many publications including the *Orange County Register*, the *Los Angeles Times*, the *Harvard Review Communication Newsletter*, *Forbes*, *American Way* magazine, the *Sacramento Bee*, *USA Today*, *The New York Times*, *Investor's Business Daily* and The Associated Press, in addition to many others.

Kerr also starred in her own one-woman show, *Out of Her Mind*, which met with great success and which she single-handedly wrote. In it she played a number of original characters.

In addition to lecturing and teaching ExecuProv courses, both in classroom situations and in private, one-on-one coaching sessions, Kerr provides speechwriting services for many of her clients. Kerr also provides her creative services to large companies for corporate comedy industrials and also offers public relations consultant services through her award-winning P.R. firm, Kerr PR.

Kerr is frequently sought out as a keynote speaker addressing presentation and communication skills and humor in the workplace.

In addition to *The Bliss or "Diss" Connection? Email Etiquette For The Business Professional,* she is the author of other books including: *Funny Business: How To Make* You *Laugh On the Job Every Day; How To Think Fast On Your Feet (Without Putting Them In Your Mouth); Death By PowerPoint: How To Avoid Killing Your Presentation and Sucking the Life Out of Your Audience; "When I Say This…Do You Mean That",* a book addressing one-on-one communication on the job; and a book on public speaking skills, *"I've Asked Miller To Say A Few Words",* as well as a book on how to get humor and good storytelling into speeches and presentations, *"What's So Funny?"* All of her books use improv comedy techniques as the basis for the lessons. She also has written a book on sketch comedy, *Build to Laugh: How to Construct Sketch Comedy with the Fast and Funny Formula; Networking Skills That Will Get You the Job You Want* and also penned her first major literary work, *Charlie's Notes, A Memoir,* the story of her father's life as a jazz musician. Many of her works have been translated in Italian, Spanish, Japanese, German and Arabic.

Cherie Kerr resides in Santa Ana, California. She is the mother of three and also has five grandchildren.

ExecuProv offers workshop sessions, seminars and private coaching to both companies and individuals worldwide. Ms. Kerr is available for keynote speeches and special appearances. Please submit a written request for any of the above to:

ExecuProv
DePietro Performance Center
809 N. Main Street
Santa Ana, CA 92701

Email: CherieKerr@aol.com
Visit ExecuProv's website: www.ExecuProv.com

Other Books By Cherie Kerr

Funny Business:
How To Make <u>You</u> Laugh On The Job Every Day

"I've Asked Miller to Say a Few Words" *—New and Exciting Ways to Improve Speaking and Presentation Skills Through the Use of Improvisational Comedy Techniques*
Foreword by Phil Hartman

"What's So Funny?" *—How to Get Good Storytelling and Humor Into Your Speeches and Presentations*

"When I Say This...," **"Do You Mean That?"** *— Enhancing On-The-Job Communications Skills Using the Rules and Tools of The Improv Comedy Player*
Foreword by Julia Sweeney

How To Think Fast On Your Feet (Without Putting Them In Your Mouth)
For The Business Professional Who Doesn't Know What To Say When...

Death By Powerpoint:
How To Avoid Killing Your Presentation and Sucking the Life Out of Your Audience

Build to Laugh:
How To Construct Sketch Comedy With The Fast and Funny Formula

Charlie's Notes: A Memoir

Coming Soon

Wit's End: *How To Deal With Difficult People*

I would like to order the following books:

_____

_____

_____

Name _____

Address _____

City _____

State _____ Zip _____

Telephone No. _____ Fax No. _____

Email Address _____

Credit Card _____ Visa _____ MasterCard

Credit Card No. _____

Expiration Date _____

Signature _____

_____ Please put me on your email list to be informed of upcoming classes held at the DePietro Performance Center.

Please Mail order forms to :

ExecuProv Press
809 N. Main Street
Santa Ana, CA 92701

Kerr's books are also available at Amazon.com, Barnes&Noble.com and at all major bookstores throughout the country.